IMAGES OF ENGLAND

Letchworth
Garden City

Aerial view of Letchworth, 1937. At this period the sinews of the plan stood out in sharp relief, revealing the lop-sided and sporadic development of the town centre.

IMAGES OF ENGLAND

Letchworth Garden City

Mervyn Miller

NONSUCH

The young pioneers, Edward and Peggy Unwin c.1908. Wearing woollens, tweeds, and sandals, handmade by George Adams from Derbyshire, these two children typify the spirit of adventure during the early development of Letchworth. Their father, Raymond Unwin, prepared the layout plan of Letchworth Garden City.

To the memory of my father, Thomas Miller, died 24 September 1995

First published 1995
This new pocket edition 2005
Images unchanged from first edition

Nonsuch Publishing Limited
The Mill, Brimscombe Port,
Stroud, Gloucestershire, GL5 2QG
www.nonsuch-publishing.com

British Library Cataloguing in Publication Data.
A catalogue record for this book is available from the British Library.

ISBN 1-84588-157-5

Typesetting and origination by Nonsuch Publishing Limited
Printed in Great Britain by Oaklands Book Services Limited

Contents

Acknowledgments

I should like to thank Bob Lancaster, Curator of the First Garden City Heritage Museum, William Heaton Vice-Chairman of the Letchworth Garden City Society, Sarah Carrick of the Letchworth Garden City Corporation, David Brightwell of the Howard Cottage Society and all who provided material and assistance for this book. The illustrations on pages 118, 119(bottom), 120(top) were provided by *North Herts Gazette*; pages 119(top) and 120(bottom) by *Letchworth Comet*; pages 105(bottom), 116(top and bottom), 127, by the Howard Cottage Society, and the remainder in Section Seven by Letchworth Garden City Corporation. Sheila Murray greatly eased the process of editing and processing the introduction and captions.

Introduction

'Town and Country must be married, and out of this joyous union will spring a new hope, a new life, a new civilisation'. So wrote Ebenezer Howard (1850-1928) in his book, *Tomorrow: A Peaceful Path to Real Reform*, published in 1898, in which the concept of the Garden City was set out in detail. A long-time Parliamentary reporter, Howard had been impressed with the dissatisfaction of all shades of political opinion with the social and environmental consequences of the Victorian Industrial conurbations, and the depressed state of agriculture, which hastened the migration to towns. Howard was well aware of the model communities promoted by enlightened industrialists such as W.H. Lever, at Port Sunlight (1888) and George Cadbury at Bournville (1895), and of a stream of Utopian thought including Robert Owen's *New Lanark* and Edward Bellamy's *Looking Backward*, a vision of Boston, Massachusetts in 2000 AD, transformed by advanced technology. Although he later rejected Bellamy's centralised bureaucracy, the book became the catalyst which stimulated Howard to formulate his own 'unique combination of proposals', in which the Garden City became the means of reforming society as a whole.

Boldly combining the strengths and eliminating the weaknesses of both urban and rural life, the 'The Magnets' diagram indicated that, given a real choice, the people would flock to the Garden City. Howard envisaged that a cluster of six Garden Cities would evolve, each with a population of 32,000, and contained within a rural zone or green belt. Local employment, social services and recreation would be provided within each, but they would eventually interact with a larger central city of 58,000, forming a 'Social City' of 250,000 population. Howard, who was a compulsive inventor drew precise diagrams to show circular cities, subdivided into wards by radial boulevards, with a Central Park, flanked by civic and religious buildings, a vast circular covered shopping centre - the Crystal Palace, and quadrangles and curved crescents of housing. Industry, which would benefit from electric power to eliminate pollution, was to be located around the rim of the settlement, on a circumferential railway. The Garden City would be developed by a private company, who would purchase the site of 6,000 acres, developing the central 1,000 for the settlement itself, with the remainder retained for agriculture and recreation. In the 1890s there was no planning legislation to restrict use of agricultural land for urban purposes. Periodic revaluation of the estate would enable further capital to be raised until the Garden City was complete. The constitution of the company would ensure a dividend limitation to shareholders, and provision for surpluses to returned to the residents.

Initially dismissed as 'Utopian scheming', a core of Howard's supporters formed the Garden City Association in 1899, determined to promote his vision of 'an ideal city made practicable'. In 1901, the recruitment of Thomas Adams (1870-1940) as the Association's Secretary (later to be the Estate Manager at Letchworth and the first President of the Town Planning Institute in 1914), and Ralph Neville KC (1865-1930) as the Association's Chairman, did much to boost the credibility of the nascent Garden City Movement. After national conferences held at Bournville in 1901 and Port Sunlight in 1902, a Garden City pioneer company was formed, charged with finding and purchasing a suitable site for development; many options were examined but, 'Letchford Manor nr Hitchin' emerged as front-runner in Summer 1903. Although only 1014 acres, the Association's Solicitor Herbert Warren, and his clerk James Brown, astutely negotiated options to purchase 3818 acres from 15 owners, at a cost of £155,387. First Garden City Ltd was registered on 1 September 1903, with Ralph Neville as Chairman. On 9 October, guests of the Association crowded into a marquee to escape pouring rain on what is now Letchworth Cricket Ground, to hear Earl Grey declare the estate open, congratulating Howard 'that within five short years his visionary hopes for tomorrow have become the almost fulfilled realisation of today'.

Much work was required to confirm Grey's plaudit. Criss-crossed by the Cambridge branch of the Great Northern Railway, the Hitchin-Baldock Road, the historic Icknield Way, and Wilbury Road, and a handful of lanes and tracks, the area included the villages of Norton in the north-east, Willian in the south, with a handful of cottages around the historic St Mary's church, which stood on guard in front of the Tudor Letchworth Hall. An Engineering Committee was convened to obtain a water supply, to build roads, and obtain a layout plan. In October 1903, a limited competition was organised on an ad hoc basis, with entries from W.R. Lethaby and Halsey Ricardo, Barry Parker and Raymond Unwin, and the Hitchin architect Geoffry Lucas, with Sidney Cranfield. After assessment, which included consultation of the GNR, the Parker and Unwin plan was provisionally approved on 28 February 1904, and confirmed as 'the Company's Plan' on 11 February.

Barry Parker (1867-1947) and Raymond Unwin (1863-1940) were brothers-in-law, followers of William Morris and the Arts and Crafts Movement, who had commenced practice in Buxton, Derbyshire in 1896. Unwin's interest in working-class housing stemmed from his duties for the Staveley Coal and Iron Company of Chesterfield. Unwin had met Howard at Bournville in 1901, and was determined to obtain the Letchworth commission, lodging for six weeks on site, examining all natural and landscape features of the site to incorporate them sympathetically into his plan. The three oak trees at the head of the present Broadway enabled him to fix the axial line which is such a striking feature of the plan. The formal framework reflected the precision of Howard's diagrams, and Wren's plan for rebuilding the City of London, but there was ample scope for informal details and housing groups to be included as implementation progressed. The Pix Valley was preserved as Howard Park, Norton Common became the major recreation area for the town, and the industrial area was located east of the town centre, along the railway, with several early factories served by private sidings.

Purchase of the estate, and construction of the roads stretched the Company's finances, yet basic infrastructure was required to attract industrialists and housebuilders. In 1905, Thomas Adams, in conjunction with two publishers, organised the Cheap Cottage Exhibition, in which plots between the railway and Norton Common, along Norton Way North and Wilbury Road were leased to developers who constructed cottages at a cost of £150, a figure which would provide a 5% return based on the rent level affordable by an agricultural or industrial labourer. The 114 exhibits attracted 60,000 visitors during the summer to witness 'Garden City in the making'. A number of technically advanced buildings included the concrete 'Round House' and 158 Wilbury Road. Housing Societies - the Garden City Tenants, Letchworth Cottages and Buildings, and in 1911, the Howard Cottage Society, named after Ebenezer Howard, began to construct the simple pebbledashed tile-roofed housing groups set in generous gardens, for which Letchworth became famous. In 1919, Garden City designs were made the basis of the national Housing Act which introduced Local Authority housing throughout England. Individual houses proliferated, the best influenced by Arts and Crafts designs, by Parker and Unwin, M.H. Baillie Scott, Bennett and Bidwell, and Courtenay Crickmer. Overall, Letchworth contributed significantly to setting 20th century housing and environmental standards. The pioneer lifestyle, particularly the free-thinking vegetarian middle-classes, who rejected alcohol, and wore smocks and sandals, became a subject for satire, both locally and nationally. 'The Cloisters', built by the formidable Miss Lawrence, epitomised the idyllic nature of early Garden City life.

The reality was more mundane, if pragmatic. Letchworth was an industrial town, and the attraction of engineering, woodworking, and printing firms was a key to its success. An early coup was the attraction of Dents, the publishers, to a prominent site on Works Road, where the famous Everyman Edition was printed by the million. In 1910, the Spirella Company, an American firm which had patented spiral wound springs as corset stiffeners, located in the 'sheds', legacy of the 1905 exhibition and a host of other uses, and proceeded to construct an enormous factory, designed by Cecil Hignett, completed in three stages between 1912 and 1922. 'Castle Corset' dominated female employment as surely as its form loomed above the railway cutting north of the town centre. During the First World War, two Belgian refugees Georges Kryn and Raoul Lahy, formed a munitions factory, 'K & L', which brought heavy engineering to Letchworth. In 1920, the British Tabulating Machine Co Ltd acquired a large site on Icknield Way, and their punched card data processors laid the basis for computer manufacture. The town centre developed slowly, with piecemeal shopping parades along Station road and Leys Avenue, with The Colonnade at the head the dominant building until the construction of the Garden City Company's offices in 1912-13, and the Midland Bank in 1922-3. The Georgian style was adopted for Broadway, which was intermittently developed, with Eastcheap becoming the major shopping street. The Town Square (now J.F. Kennedy Gardens) was laid out in 1914 and Lombardy poplars were planted to outline a group of civic and religious buildings 'modelled on the work of Wren and other masters', destined never to be constructed.

Letchworth was acutely conscious of its visual image from its inception. Pictorial guides and brochures proliferated, and an amazing range of postcards appeared. Through the lenses of the early photographers we can revisit the town which resembled a pioneer camp, experience the freshness of the newly built housing areas and tree-lined streets before the car reigned supreme, visit 'The Cloisters', witness May Day, with Ebenezer Howard in costume, see the women of Spirella hard at work, or the Kinora men at their tea break, the children at Norton School, or recreation of the first open-air swimming bath, or in the British Tab cycle club ...

Letchworth grew steadily if slowly, promoted by First Garden City Ltd, with the benign acquiescence of the Letchworth Parish Council, and from 1919, Letchworth Urban District Council. After 1945, everything changed. Statutory town-planning gave the local authority far greater control of development, resources were channelled into council and overspill housing, private development was inhibited by taxes on the development value of land. When controls on the latter were lifted, however, the First Garden City Ltd became an attractive takeover target. Letchworth UDC successfully promoted a private Bill through Parliament, which vested the assets of the Company, including the freehold of the site, in the Letchworth Garden City Corporation, which began operations on 1 January 1963. Since that date, the Corporation managed the estate in accordance with the principles of Howard's original model, updated as necessary. From 1974, the local authority became the North Hertfordshire District Council, expanded to include Hitchin, Baldock, Royston, and the rural hinterland. From the 1980s, many outworn industrial sites were redeveloped, and a large business park built south of the old K&L site. New housing had been built beyond the earlier limits, notably Lordship and Manor Farm, and Jackman's Estates, either side of Letchworth Gate, the pre-war link to the Great North Road. Happily, the town centre, and many of the early housing areas are now a Conservation Area. The renewed emphasis on heritage is reflected in the reconstitution of the Corporation as the Letchworth Heritage Foundation, as of 1 October 1995, charged with taking Howard's Garden City beyond the millenium towards its centenary in 2003. With the First Garden City Heritage Museum, firmly established in the old Parker and Unwin offices on Norton Way South, increasing interest in all aspects of Letchworth, and the vigilance of voluntary bodies such as the Letchworth Garden City Society, it is evident that the idealism which created the Garden City is still present in the community.

Dr Mervyn Miller
September 1995

One

An Ideal City made Practicable

The unassuming revoluntionary. The rather
bland persona of Ebenezer Howard (1850-
1928) peers out from the frontispiece of *Garden
Cities of To-morrow*, the popular third edition
of Howard's original book, published in 1902.
It would be nice to know the origin of the
inscription.

The 'Three Magnets', 1898, in which
Howard summarised the argument for
the Garden City with his 'town-country
magnet' which would eliminate the
disadvantages of Victorian overcrowded
cities and depopulated countryside.

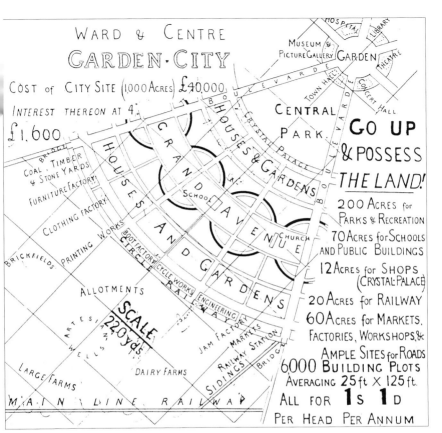

Ward and centre of the Garden City (before 1898). A diagram drawn by Howard himself which includes the biblical exhortation 'Go up and possess the land!', perhaps wisely omitted from the published version.

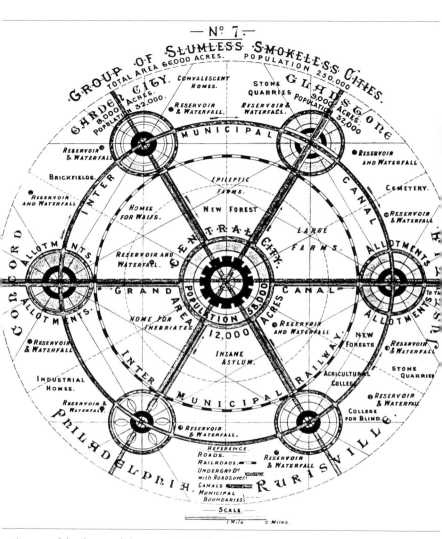

A group of slumless, smokeless cities, 1898. The Garden City cluster represented the ultimate achievement of Howard's concept. Today the location of Stevenage New Town and Welwyn Garden City along the same motorway and rail corridor as Letchworth represents a partial fulfilment of Howard's prophesy. In 1967, the cluster theory was chosen as the basis of the plan for Milton Keynes, the last major State-promoted New Town.

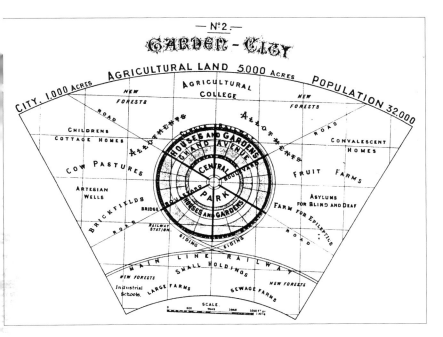

GARDEN - CITY

CITY. 1,000 ACRES · AGRICULTURAL LAND 5,000 ACRES · POPULATION 32,000

NEW FORESTS · AGRICULTURAL COLLEGE · NEW FORESTS

ROAD · ALLOTMENTS · ROAD

CHILDRENS COTTAGE HOMES · HOUSES AND GARDENS · CONVALESCENT HOMES

GRAND AVENUE

COW PASTURES · BOULEVARD · CENTRAL PARK · BOULEVARD · FRUIT FARMS

ARTESIAN WELLS · ASYLUMS FOR BLIND AND DEAF

BRICKFIELDS · HOUSES AND GARDENS · FARM FOR EPILEPTICS

BRIDGE · ROAD

RAILWAY STATION · SIDING · SIDING · ROAD

MAIN LINE RAILWAY

NEW FORESTS · SMALL HOLDINGS · NEW FORESTS

Industrial Schools · LARGE FARMS · SEWAGE FARMS

SCALE.
0 · 920 · 1940 · 5280 FT OR 1 MILE

Above: The Garden City in its agricultural belt. Only 1,000 acres out of 6,000 was to be developed for the settlement itself. At Letchworth the estate was smaller, 3,018 acres, and the urban area was expanded in the interwar period to account for smaller households. The principle of an agricultural green belt predated modern planning legislation.

Right: The 1902 re-issue of Howard's book under its better-known title *Garden Cities of Tomorrow* featured this attractive cover drawing by the Socialist artist, Walter Crane, a friend of William Morris.

Above: The Letchworth estate had been purchased in summer 1903. On 9 October, crowds in the marquee listen to Earl Grey declaring the Garden City estate open. It poured with rain while guests made their way through the mud to and from the temporary station 1½ miles away.

Left: The Board of Directors of the development company, First Garden City Ltd, was chaired by Ralph Neville, centre, and included Ebenezer Howard, centre right.

BOARD of DIRECTORS
FIRST GARDEN CITY LIMITED

The Hon. Mr Justice Neville, whose portrait occupies the central space has been compelled, by reason of his appointment to be one of his Majesty's Judges, to retire from his position as a Director, and the Chairmanship of the Board of Directors of First Garden City Limited. He still retains his interest in the scheme and will continue to act as Chairman of the Council of the Garden City Association.

Letchworth Corner, at the junction of the Hitchin and Baldock Roads with Letchworth Lane and Spring Road, was the most tangible early landmark in the Garden City. The old Tudor cottage was the local post office, where Raymond Unwin lodged when preparing his layout plan. In the 1920s, the house was restored and embellished as 'Scudemore', and remains a well-known landmark. In this photograph from around 1908 the postman sits astride his tricycle, with its wicker basket for parcels.

Later, the ornamental estate cottage on the corner of Spring Road became the post office, which continues to this day. In this attractive 1930s view the traffic along the Hitchin-Baldock Road has not built up to any great extent.

The majestic elms and venerable hedgerows lined Letchworth Lane as it led down towards old Letchworth.

On the right were Manor Farm cottages, which still survive today. The tall elm trees on the left hand side have, however, been replaced by the Manor Housing estate. Cattle certainly could not roam safely along the lane as shown in this photograph taken in the early 1920s.

The tiny twelfth-century St Mary's church, only 60 ft long internally, reflected the small size and remoteness of Letchworth Manor.

Looking back from Letchworth Hall towards St Mary's, the view is dominated by the tall elms which all but hide the tiny church in this pre-1914 view.

Letchworth Hall, seen here in the early 1930s, dates from the fifteenth and sixteenth centuries, but has been greatly enlarged. In 1904 it became a hotel and welcomed its first guests for Christmas.

The parkland to the west of the hall was laid out as a golf course, initially nine, but later the full eighteen holes, with the advice of Harry Vardon, a famous professional. In 1920, smart plus-fours and flannels were the order of the day, with boys as caddies to carry the clubs.

The pastoral charm of Willian Village, with its pond, and the Fox Inn, are evident in this fine pre-1914 view.

A few yards away, the Wymondley turn shows the lack of traffic, the muddy lanes, with a pool from the overflow of the pond, and thatched cottages in the background which have since disappeared. The priest in clerical cape could be Father Adrian Fortescue of St Hugh's church, Pixmore Way.

Norton Village is of Saxon origin, and prospered as a farming community from the seventeenth century. The attractive thatched cottages to the left, seen here c. 1908, still survive, but the pond on the right, and the elms which conceal Manor Farm, now converted to old peoples flats, have long since disappeared, and the road is now heavily trafficked.

As late as the 1930s, little has changed, apart from the road being made up. The Three Horseshoes is still a popular hostelry, but the backdrop of tall elms disappeared in the 1960s and '70s through Dutch Elm Disease. A canvas topped lorry and a distant pony and trap are the only visible traffic.

The cattle sheds and pens at Manor Farm, Willian, pre-1914. Pride of place was given to the bulls 'Duke of Puddington' and 'Burton Primax'

Harvest home 1914, with threshing machinery and a steam-driven traction engine. Much of the Garden City estate remained in agricultural use for many years and the fields along what is now the central section of Broadway produced abundant crops during the First World War.

The Parker and Unwin families in the garden of 'Moorlands' Buxton, c. 1898. Raymond Unwin stands in the back row at the extreme left, and Barry Parker at the extreme right. Parker's parents are seated in the wicker chairs, while in front, to the right sits Ethel Unwin (née Parker), with the young Edward Unwin, already clad in flannel smock and sandals, in the centre. To the left of Barry Parker is his younger brother Stanley, who lived on Wilbury Road, Letchworth, and was well-remembered as a skilled craftsman and teacher at the St Christopher School.

Opposite above: Almost immediately Letchworth became a popular venue for outings and conferences. This group arrived at Whitsun 1904 to tour the estate under the guidance of Raymond Unwin.

Opposite below: In 1905, an extensive agricultural conference was organised by the Estate Manager Thomas Adams. He sits centre right, alongside Ebenezer Howard, with a young girl on his knee, and to his left, H. Rider Haggard the famous novelist, who took an active interest in agricultural matters. On the back row, towards the left of the picture can be seen Barry Parker, in boater hat, and Raymond Unwin, characteristically dressed in a tweed suit

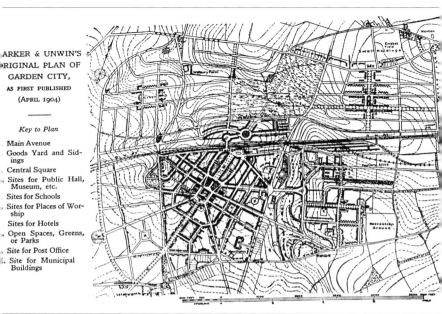

ARKER & UNWIN'S
ORIGINAL PLAN OF
GARDEN CITY,
AS FIRST PUBLISHED
(APRIL 1904)

Key to Plan

Main Avenue
Goods Yard and Sidings
Central Square
Sites for Public Hall, Museum, etc.
Sites for Schools
Sites for Places of Worship
Sites for Hotels
Open Spaces, Greens, or Parks
Site for Post Office
Site for Municipal Buildings

'The Company's Plan' April 1904. This plan, preserved in the First Garden City Heritage Museum, was carefully drawn up on linen for publication in connection with fundraising for the development of Letchworth. Although detail, particularly in the outlying housing areas, was modified, the plan endured as the overall layout for the First Garden City for many years. Visible in the centre are the axial line of Broadway, with, to the right, Norton Way shown as 'North Road'. There was a tentative proposal to divert traffic away from Baldock through Letchworth to encourage its development. Thank goodness that never happened!

Two

Garden City in the Making

In the winter of 1905, unemployed labourers were brought in from London to build the first network of roads around the infant Garden City. They were housed in the sheds which were built for the Cheap Cottage Exhibition. The workmen pose in front of their temporary Garden City home. The rolled-up sleeves indicate that the photograph was taken shortly before their return home the following spring.

In 1904, Alpha Cottages, the first new Garden City homes, were completed. The workmen from Picton and Hope pose on wooden scaffolding in front of the nearly completed block. On 7 July 1904, Miss Elizabeth H. Revill moved into No 1 Alpha Cottages, the first resident of a purpose-built house in Letchworth.

S 13666 Letchworth Garden City (North East)

Letchworth resembled a giant building site for many years. The Cheap Cottage Exhibition of 1905 was the first extensive housing area to be developed. The main sites lay between the railway and Norton Common. From the roof of the shops adjoining 'The Peoples House' in Station Road in the early 1920s, there is a fine view over the station towards the cottages along Nevells (formerly Exhibition) Road. In the background are Norton Common, Norton Way North, and the extensive Norton Glebe housing.

VIEW. NORTON WAY NORTH. LETCHWORTH.

In 1914, looking north along Norton Way North, shortly after its connection through the railway embankment was made, the newly completed houses along Glebe Road can be seen.

Looking north from Ridge Road about 1910, across the part-completed factories along Works Road, Norton Way North, towards the housing in Glebe Road, under construction. In the foreground, the children seem to have found a fine playground on the muddy field which would later be developed with the factories fronting Pixmore Avenue.

A bird's eye view c. 1912 from the newly completed first wing of the Spirella factory. In the foreground are the sheds, which had served as Spirella's first Letchworth base. Beyond are The Quadrant and Nevells Road, with the 1905 Cheap Cottages, and, on the distant horizon, Norton Glebe.

Market gardeners pose against the truncated Norton Way North, with Exhibition Road (now Nevells Road) leading upwards and flanked by the 1905 Cheap Cottages. The hip-roofed bungalow marks Cross Street. The lack of building on the left of the picture confirms that this view pre-dates construction of The Skittles Inn in 1907.

Icknield Way, facing Norton Common, provided an attractive setting for the 1905 Cheap Cottages. On the right, the corner cottage had become almost completely covered by vegetation prior to its restoration in the late 1980s.

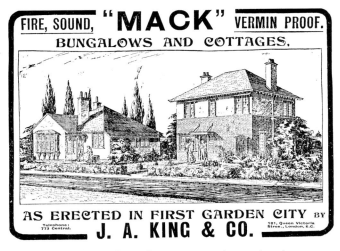

In the 1905 Exhibition, the emphasis was on novel materials and constructional methods. This house and bungalow, constructed in Nevells Road, featured vermin-proof walling materials, as advertised in the Exhibition catalogue.

THE COTTAGE BATH OF THE CENTURY.

The inclusion of a bath was a requirement of the Exhibition, but not necessarily in a special bathroom. Some cottages featured baths in the kitchen or scullery, beneath a worktop, and one or two even included this patent bath which would fold away into a cupboard alongside the kitchen range.

The Quadrant took the axial line of Broadway towards Norton Common. Developed with cottages for the 1905 Exhibition, it included an entry promoted by Bournville Tenants, from Cadburys' Model Village. The street was originally planted with pear trees which can be seen in the roadside verge.

As they matured, the pears made a magnificent showing at blossom time, as did many of the ornamental species planted in the Garden City. The reverse of this 1920s postcard records that the pear trees were destroyed in October 1929: the reason is not known.

'The Nook Cottage' on the corner of Cross Street and Icknield Way was one of the most charming of the 1905 exhibits with its rustic porch complete with fitted settles. The architect was George Clare, and the postcard was issued to promote the timber preservative used inside and out.

These unusual cottages on Birds Hill were among the few group designs exhibited in 1905. They were built for Heatly Gresham, an engineering firm which made bodies for London taxi cabs, and designed by the architect V. Dunkerley. The distinctive mansard roofs gave rise to the nickname 'Noah's Ark cottages'. They were successfully refurbished in the early 1980s.

A few exhibits were constructed on Wilbury Road, facing south across Norton Common. About 1906, the verges appear to have been affected by drought. On the right hand side is No 158 Wilbury Road, (see below), and next to it, a timber-clad cottage by A.H. Clough of Ringwood Hampshire, whose nephew, the architect, Clough Williams-Ellis supervised construction.

No 158 Wilbury Road was perhaps the most revolutionary of the 1905 Exhibition Cottages. Designed by John Brodie, the Liverpool City Engineer, it still looks surprisingly modern today. This photograph, taken in 1975, shows how well the building survived.

These photographs show how 158 Wilbury Road was built. At the top, the operatives are taking the storey-height concrete panels out of wooden moulds. The panels were manufactured in a quarry near Liverpool, and the middle view shows them being assembled to check on the fit. Notice that the window frames are already in place. In the bottom view, the panels have been taken apart and loaded on to railway wagons for their journey to Letchworth. They were hauled uphill from the railway sidings on horse-drawn wagons, and the building was re-assembled for the last time.

Right: Further along Wilbury Road, 'The Round House', No 140, was also constructed from concrete panels. Its name derived from its 16-sided plan, and it had weird wedge-shaped rooms radiating from a central roof-lit hall. It survived until the mid 1980s, when it literally crumbled away when being taken apart for intended re-erection at Standalone Farm. In this early picture, the owner stands in the doorway, and prolific roses soften the stark outline of the building.

Below: These plans from the Cheap Cottage catalogue show the unusual form of the building.

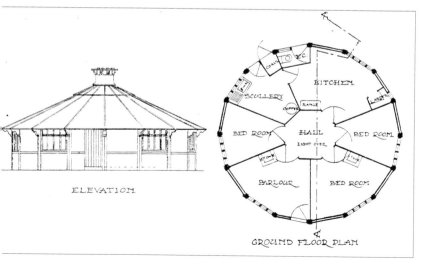

ELEVATION

GROUND FLOOR PLAN

Eastholm Green was built in 1905-6, and largely designed by Parker and Unwin. On the left is part of the distinctive angled block which 'turns the corner' to Wilbury Road. The character of the green was disrupted when Eastern Way was cut through in the late 1940s to give access to the Grange Estate.

Westholm Green, facing Norton Common, also by Parker and Unwin, was a self-contained cottage development by Garden City Tenants, a housing society which built modest rental accommodation for industrial workers in Letchworth. The group had its own central green, and the approaches were originally closed off by gates, as can be seen at the left. A road was eventually cut through and around the green for motor vehicles in the late 1950s, and the houses are now privately owned.

The railway initially provided a barrier between the two halves of the Garden City Estate. Access was restricted to narrow 'cattle creeps' which led beneath the embankment. This one, infilled about 1913, led from Station Road along what is now the car park of 'The Settlement' to Exhibition (now Nevells) Road. Another cattle creep still exists on Spring Road and vehicular through-traffic has recently been restricted.

In 1913, a bridge was built to connect Norton Way North and Norton Way South. A Great Northern Railway goods engine pauses co-operatively on the bridge just past the long-vanished signal box. A horse-drawn Italian ice cream cart waits in Nevells Road. The tall telegraph pole indicates the unsightly wirescape which accompanied the spread of the telephone network in its early years.

The railway bridge became a favourite vantage point for photographs looking south along Norton Way. In 1913, shortly after completion of the bridge, a group of children walk boldly down the middle of the road, leaving a lone toddler on the crossroads where Works Road and Station Road branch off. The foreground trees have just been planted, while the sites at either side remain undeveloped. On the right are the Garden City Hotel, and the old St Michael's church, both now demolished, while in the far background on the left, is the Girls Club wing of the Howard Memorial Hall.

In 1935, the Howard Park corner shopping parades at either side of the road have been built, the foreground verge-side planting in has disappeared, while the street trees along Norton Way South itself have all but concealed the buildings. Traffic includes a single decker bus about to cross Norton Way into Station Road.

In 1907, a further Cottage Exhibition was held, with its site largely along Lytton Avenue between Gernon Road and Pixmore Way. The entrance to the exhibition site is at the left, with a kiosk advertising building materials on the right. In the centre are the exhibits, largely semi-detached and grouped cottages, all of which survive to the present.

The information kiosk was later incorporated into an unusual house, which served as a studio and even a knitting factory. To the right, Gernon Road is barely more than a muddy track, devoid of development where Commerce Avenue was built in the 1920s, and the North Herts District Council offices were to be constructed in the early 1970s.

Norton Way South was the principal road in Letchworth prior to the construction of the full length of Broadway. In the centre of this 1908 view is No 298 Norton Way South, which almost conceals the thatched offices of Parker and Unwin, now the First Garden City Heritage Museum. On the extreme left, far away, stands the Mrs Howard Memorial Hall. On the right, the connecting link of Pixmore Way to the Baldock Road has not yet been constructed.

Near its junction with Baldock Road, Norton Way South was developed with a block of houses promoted by Ebenezer Howard himself, who lived at the second from the left, No 359, until 1911. The architects were Parker and Unwin. The wayside bench in the centre of this 1908 picture has long since disappeared.

Albeit the main road from Hitchin to Cambridge, Baldock Road was quiet and traffic-free before the First World War. In this Clutterbuck photograph, the only traffic is a far-distant horse and cart. The mature trees pre-dated the development of Letchworth. All the houses on the left were built before 1908-9.

Even in the 1930s, little traffic disturbed the tranquil scene. To the right is the improved line of the road, made as early as 1906. The green to the left, shaded by the poplar trees still remains a pleasant feature. This later Clutterbuck photograph, characteristically includes children in the foreground.

Most houses along the Hitchin Road between Spring Road and Broadway were built before the First World War. One of the earliest was Briarside Cottage (now Netherton), a fine Parker and Unwin house of 1906, built of a cost of just over £500. The tall elms in the foreground, and middle distance, were characteristic of the estate, and remained until the 1970s.

Looking westward along Hitchin Road, a pair of original estate cottages is on the left hand side, marking the junction with Letchworth Lane. To the right of the magnificent tree screen can be seen the double gable of Arana, a fine house designed by Courtenay Crickmer in 1907-8.

Broadway, between the Sollershotts and Town Square (J.F. Kennedy Gardens), was not made up until 1924. This view shows the cinder path which led along the grand axis of the plan into the town centre. The magnificent double avenue of lime trees has been planted in advance of the construction works.

The roundabout at the junction of the Sollershotts and Broadway, hiding behind the trees in the centre, was one of the first purpose-designed traffic gyratories. It was opened on a hot summer day in 1910 when many of the waiting cars overheated. This view dates from the late 1930s.

Broadwater Avenue took its name from the traditional 'hundred' of the county in which Letchworth is situated. In this 1912 view, the linked houses at the junction with Station Way have just been completed, but the land in the distance remained undeveloped until construction of housing in Burnell Rise and Campers Road commenced during the First World War.

Burnell Rise faces the railway which runs in a cutting to the left of the picture. The housing was constructed partly by the Howard Cottage Society, and the area became known as 'Little Belgium' during the First World War due to the number of refugee families accommodated. In the middle distance of this 1923 view, the newly-completed Spirella factory, 'Castle Corset', dominates its surroundings, and development along Icknield Way and Bedford Road would not begin until the 1930s.

A 1923 view eastwards along Baldock Road with the Jackmans Place council housing estate, built 1919-21, designed by Bennett and Bidwell. In the woodland to the left was the Letchworth Hospital, the site of which was redeveloped in the 1980s for the Garden House Hospice. Pixmore Way can be seen at the extreme left, but as yet there is no connection to Letchworth Gate at the right. The absence of traffic contrasts sharply with the present, with its speed-monitoring cameras.

In the south-west of Letchworth, the Hitchin Road led down Rosehill towards 'Sleepy Hollow', the early nickname for Hitchin. In this 1923 view there is a total absence of traffic, with the telegraph poles providing only visually disruptive features.

Pixmore Way became the main link to the town centre from the Baldock Road, lined with houses built by Letchworth UDC, designed by Courtenay Crickmer, 1919-21. The trees in the middle distance mark the Pix Valley and Howard Park, and beyond, the road crosses Norton Way and rises into the Town Square (J.F. Kennedy Gardens).

Letchworth Gate was constructed in the early 1930s to provide an improved link to the Great North Road. In its newly completed state, a lone limousine pauses at the kerbside. In the background, the roofs of the Jackmans Place estate can be seen. The land to the right of the road was developed for the Jackmans housing estate in the 1950s and 1960s under a scheme to house London overspill.

Three

Around the Town Centre

Topping out. First Garden City Ltd built an imposing frontage to its single storey estate office in 1913, designed by Barry Parker and Raymond Unwin. The Clerk of Works and contractors' men are gathered round the cupola which crowns the roofscape, for the traditional 'topping out' ceremony.

Broadway was designed as the principal thoroughfare leading to the station. About 1916, looking from the roof of the estate office, the first phase of the Post Office is visible at left, and centre right, the Police Station and Court, Boys Club, and the imposing Primitive Methodist Church. In the background is the Town Square, with its bandstand. Far away is Sollershott West, and on the extreme right, Broadwater Avenue, and Spring Road with 'Little Belgium'.

Looking north from the Town Square, the broadwalk, originally designed to accommodate a tramway, is in the centre of Broadway. At the left, is the Primitive Methodist church, with the Boys Club in front; at the right, the post office and Estate Office. In the far distant centre is the station, opened in 1913.

Station Place, looking towards Spirella, about 1918. A motor bus stands outside 'The Colonnade', one of the earliest shopping parades. Behind can be seen the chimney of the manager's flat above Barclays Bank. In the centre, only the first phase of Spirella has been completed, visible across the railway cutting, spanned only by a pedestrian bridge. To the right is the handsome Arts and Crafts booking office of the permanent station, built by the Great Northern Railway in 1913.

Looking from Spirella across the newly completed Neville Bridge, opened in 1930, from Spirella, the major town centre buildings are visible in the background, notably the estate office with its rooftop cupola and the newly constructed National Provincial Bank linking it to The Colonnade. To the left, Midland Bank Parade was completed in 1923-4, and far left, the station booking office.

The corner site between Station Road and Leys Avenue was originally occupied by an open market, seen here in 1908, with its open stalls and muddy ground. In the centre, boys play nonchalantly on a handcart.

The same view in the early 1930s shows 'The Peoples' House' to the left and Midland Bank Parade to the right, a fine Classical composition designed by the local architects Bennett and Bidwell. The motorbus in front is part of the regular service to Hitchin and Luton which began shortly before the First World War.

Station Road was the earliest shopping street to be developed. The earliest shops, including Cullip's General Store, Ansell's Butchery, Bradshaw's Ironmongery, and Beddoe's Confectionery and Newsagents, opened in 1906-7.

In this view of Station Road from Norton Way, Clutterbuck has, as usual, posed two children in the foreground. One of the little girls stands on the grating of the drain in the muddy gutter. In the background, the Central Hotel survived until the early 1980s; beyond Silver Birch Cottages appear very much as they do today, following their refurbishment. To the right, the Garden City Nursery has long since disappeared.

Leys Avenue became the principal shopping street before the First World War. This fine parade was designed by Bennett and Bidwell in 1908, and W.H. Smith still occupies the same shop as in 1913. Moss's, beyond was a branch of a well-known Hitchin grocers.

The lower end of Leys Avenue about 1923. The hustle and bustle of the town centre has grown, with pedestrians, bicyclists, and a horse and trap. The gabled building, right, built 1909, includes Spinks's Drapery, for many years a well-known store. In the distance are the imposing Georgian parades including The Arcade. The buildings have changed little in the intervening 70 years.

Ebenezer Howard had always stressed the value of co-operation. The Garden City Co-operators opened their store in Leys Avenue in 1907. Crowds standing in the unmade street pressed forward to the windows of the new store. In the background are shops in Station Road under construction.

Home delivery was a feature of most of the important shops in Letchworth. The Garden City Co-operators moved to larger premises in Eastcheap in 1913. Their delivery driver, with his horse-drawn van, poses in one of the many rural backwaters of the Garden City.

The Eastcheap stores soon developed a fine frontage, seen here in the early 1930s. All day kerbside parking was a feature of Letchworth at a time when comparatively few residents owned cars.

Everything for household convenience is on display in the Co-operative Store in this 1925 interior view. In the centre can be seen the cable and pulley system for dispatching cash into the central cash office, a feature affectionately remembered by many older residents.

The Co-op had its own bakery and its products are featured in this fine display float, probably prepared for the 1935 Civic Week festivities.

The Co-op also had its own dairy with home delivery. In 1935, this 'moderne' style creamery was built on Letchworth Gate on the outskirts of the Garden City. It remained a local landmark for many years, before being demolished in the early 1980s, and its site has now been redeveloped with the Barratts' grouped houses.

Above: Notts of Eastcheap were established in 1909, and were bakers and confectioners who soon developed an enviable reputation throughout the district. Here Fred Nott proudly display his range of delivery vehicles, horse-drawn and manpowered, outside the newly constructed shop.

Right: Notts opened the Icknield Halls adjacent to their premises in the 1920s, but their reputation was firmly based on their bakery as this attractive advertisement from the 1935 Civic Week brochure indicates.

Bread is the staff of life

but

the life of the staff

is 'NOT' one long loaf

OUR STAFF IS FULL OF VITAMINS AND MUCH TOO BUSY
TURNING OUT THE BEST BREAD AND CONFECTIONERY
IN THE DISTRICT TO "LOAF." :: YOU GET PERFECT
SATISFACTION FROM BOTH STAFF AND GOODS AT

NOTTS

EASTCHEAP and LEYS AVENUE
LETCHWORTH   *Phone 646*

Branches at Baldock, Hitchin, Biggleswade, Sandy, Ampthill.

Above: Spinks were long known for their drapery which included lingerie. In this 1926 photograph, their display for the Civic Week Window Dressing Competition can be seen with the latest Celanese petticoats in a prominent position.

Left: Spinks also had a comprehensive menswear department with many lines as this 1933 advertisement confirms.

Opposite above: The Picture Palace, built in Eastcheap 1909, was one of the earliest purpose-built cinemas in the country. It was the first building in the town centre to have an electricity supply, while its isolated position was felt to inhibit fire damage should the highly inflammable nitrate film of the period cause a conflagration.

Opposite below: Appropriately, the Picture Palace was joined by the Fire Station shortly before the First World War. In 1924, the cinema was refronted with a Hollywood-Roman style triumphal arch. In 1930 it featured the first 'talkies' to be shown in Letchworth. At the far left is Masons Garage, with filling station, retail showrooms and repair works.

Hollywood comes to the Garden City. In 1935, there was demand for a second cinema and the Broadway was designed by Bennett and Bidwell for Howard Hurst who constructed it using a steel frame and reinforced concrete. In this evocative night-time view, the neon strips of the facade glow invitingly while the canopy advertises Swing Time, a 1936 musical starring Fred Astaire and Ginger Rogers.

Opposite above: Town Square – the vision. It was originally intended to construct formal buildings in the centre of Town Square, now the J.F. Kennedy Gardens. In 1914 this design, influenced by the Classicism of Luytens and 'modelled on the works of Wren and other masters' showing the Council Offices and principal church, was published, and the outlines of the buildings were planted out in Lombardy Poplars, which remain to this day.

Opposite below: The reality was rather more modest, if still imposing. In 1935, the Letchworth Urban District Council built its offices facing the Town Square, for long known as the Town Hall. Designed by Bennett and Bidwell, this handsome building is still part of the North Hertfordshire District Council accommodation. In the background the steel framework of the Broadway Cinema can be seen.

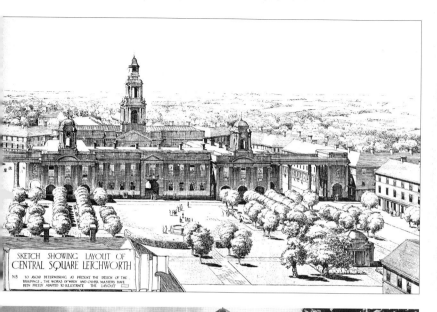

SKETCH SHOWING LAYOUT OF
CENTRAL SQUARE LETCHWORTH

N.B. TO AVOID DETERMINING AT PRESENT THE DESIGN OF THE
BUILDINGS, THE WORKS OF WREN AND OTHER MASTERS HAVE
BEEN FREELY ADAPTED TO ILLUSTRATE THE LAYOUT

The Museum was the first building on Town Square and in 1914 the ground floor was opened. The newly appointed Curator, W.P. Westell can be seen standing on the steps, with a dog under his arm.

Although lightly populated, the Garden City and its surroundings had been extensively settled by the Britons and Romans. In 1932, Westell explains about the Roman settlement nearby at Baldock and shows the artefacts to his visitors.

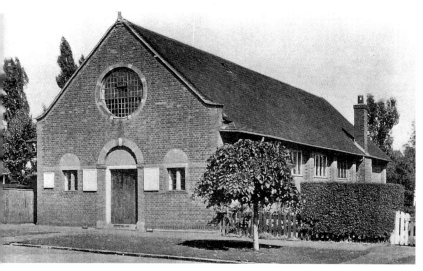

The Roman Catholic church of St Hugh of Lincoln on Pixmore Way, designed by Charles Spooner, opened in 1908, under Rev. Adrian Fortescue. The building survives but is now used as a church hall. The new church on Broadway was designed by Nicholas and Dixon Spain in 1938, but was not built until 1964.

The interior of the earlier church featured a beautiful Arts and Crafts baldachino above the high altar and Morris-style hangings.

The Free Church was opened on 17 October 1905 in a simple mission hall which cost £300. In 1907, it can be seen with the excavations for Gernon Road in the foreground, and, in the background, the Mrs Howard Memorial Hall, with the 1907 Girls Club wing under construction.

St Michael's church, Norton Way, was dedicated on 22 February 1908, and designed by Courtenay Crickmer. It was a mission church to St Mary's Letchworth. In 1919, the Rev. Kerr Olivier became Rector; his son Laurence Olivier was to become the best-acclaimed British actor of his time.

Four

At Work

Transportation of raw materials and finished goods was by rail. The Great Northern Railway constructed its sidings immediately after the foundation of Letchworth to serve the industrial estate along Works Road.

Power for industry was important too. The Gas Works was constructed early in 1905 and enlarged two years later. This photograph shows construction of the pit for the second gas holder, with the original in the background.

Some factories were imposing, such as the Lacre Motor Company which had its headquarters built on along Works Road in 1909. Finally used as a builders' merchants, this fine building was demolished in the early 1980s.

Letchworth had a number of car and vehicle builders. The Phoenix Motor Company produced high quality cars, lined up in 1911 for the photographer. Regrettably, the firm went into liquidation in 1928, and the buildings were later used as a Government Training Centre.

Printing soon became well established at Letchworth. This photograph from atound 1910 shows the compositors' room at Garden City Press, publishers of many local newspapers and brochures.

Some printing companies flourished for only a short time. This 1913 photograph shows the smouldering remains of Hayes Reynolds after a fire. The sender of the postcard records that this occured during a strike.

J.M. Dent, the London publishers, moved its activities to Letchworth in 1906 and was soon mass-producing its famous Everyman Edition in the Garden City. This photograph, c. 1910, shows the trimming shop.

Women workers at Dents parade with their bicycles, dressed as the Everyman Edition in an industrial gala in the early 1920s. Bringing up the rear is the Lacre Motor Company, and the station is in the background.

'Everything stops for tea'. Tea-time at Kinora, a short-lived manufacturer of cameras active in Letchworth before the First World War. Collars, ties and watch chains seem to have been everyday wear for many male workers.

Above: The K&L Foundry was started by Georges Kryn and Raoul Lahy, two Belgian refugees, 1915. The company was soon hard at work manufacturing armaments, which are seen stacked in the foreground.

Right: The millionth K&L shell was presented to David Lloyd George, then Minister of Munitions, later Prime Minister, remembered for his 'homes for heroes' pledge of November 1918.

In addition to armaments, K&L manufactured components for tanks, and Bailey bridges; here, one is under test at the works. Later the company diversified into manufacture of cranes.

K&L and other heavy industries were served by a private rail siding which ran through the industrial estate. Here, goods from the furniture manufacturers, Meredew, are being loaded on to a train, with the K&L office block in the background.

Winter wonderland: Dunhams Lane, flanked by mature trees, covered in hoar frost, in February 1917. The lines in the foreground belong to the siding running between Meredew to the right, and K&L to the left, neither of which can be seen in this idyllic view.

'Castle Corset', Spirella, was constructed alongside the railway. The first phase, with its well-lit workshops, between the two hip-roofed administration buildings was completed in 1912. The roof of the old station can be seen at the left above the railway cutting, while in the centre the notice board announces the construction of a pedestrian bridge across the railway.

The opening of the Spirella Gardens, 1930. Cllr. A.W. Brunt opens the gardens, while the founder of Spirella, William Wallace Kincaid, seated to the right with a rug over his knees, looks somewhat bemused, and Cllr. Charles Ball looks on rather sternly.

A girl's best friend is her sewing machine ... at least if she worked for Spirella. The workroom is a hive of activity, but Spirella provided a subsidised canteen, library, baths and other facilities for their female workforce.

The processing of the thousands of orders from all over the country demanded an enormous administration operation as can be seen in this view of the general office, dating from 1927.

Left: Fashions of 1934. A group of models, dressed in the latest Spirella corsets, poses in precise formation, as if choreographed by Busby Berkeley in one of the Hollywood musicals of the period.

Below: Callisthenics in the Spirella Ballroom, late 1920s. Greek style dancing in formation, with tunics, and bare feet, was a vogue of the period and the Spirella girls pose as if on an antique freize.

Right: The Edmundsbury Weaving Works produced high quality hand-woven textiles. Edmund Hunter brought his firm to Letchworth in 1908 to this fine purpose-designed Parker and Unwin factory in Birds Hill.

Below: Dorothea Hunter presides in the middle of the weaving shed. The Hunters were one of the first firms in Letchworth to pay for two weeks holiday, in addition to Bank Holidays, for their employees.

Left: The interior of the Drawing Office of Parker and Unwin, 296 Norton Way South is now the First Garden City Heritage Museum. In 1909, the assistants work under gaslights, the walls are lined with Parker's watercolour sketches, of his major projects, and the room is spanned with an enormous baulk of timber.

Below: The offices were completed in 1907 and thatched with water reed by craftsmen from Soham near Ely. The firm issued a postcard showing the finished building.

Telegrams: COWELL, SOHAM.   Telephone No. **016**.

Specimen of Reed Thatching, done on Architects' Offices, Garden City.

Service industries soon flourished in Letchworth, not least George Hutt, the Garden City sweep, seen here with his wife in the 1920s at a gala in Howard Park.

Listening-in to the wireless became universally popular in the interwar period and mobile servicing, particularly for fitting and adjusting aerials and recharging acumulators was in great demand. Mr Berrett of Station Road poses with his motorised tricycle in the Westbury district.

Letchworth Power Station began operation in 1907, and was periodically rebuilt. It was owned by First Garden City Ltd until Nationalisation in 1947. This 1950s view, presents a more industrial image than customary. The Power Station, with its twin cooling towers, was swept away and rebuilt in the early 1970s.

Transport for industry was a critical factor. In July 1940 an early LNER container operation, using trucks with a single front wheel, delivers bulk paper to Hollerith, which manufactured punched card data processors.

Leslie Irvin had demonstrated his parachute to the US Airforce in 1919, and founded his British subsidiary in 1926. His firm was located on Icknield Way. It was calculated that his product saved 45,000 lives in the Allied Forces during the Second World War. Here he holds a seat-harness.

The British Tabulating Machinery Company opened its factory on Icknield Way in 1921. It was designed by Cecil Hignett, architect of Spirella. It soon expanded to become an enormous building complex, and its products were precursors of modern computers. The Icknield Way premises were demolished in the early 1980s and redeveloped for housing.

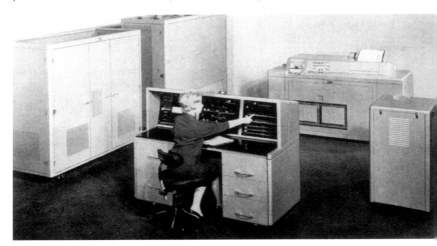

The ICT type 1202 Electronic Computer. Computers were developed after the Second World War and International Computers Ltd still have a presence in Letchworth. Their early models were extremely bulky and demanded air-conditioned rooms, and the resources of a miniature power station. The era of personal computer-word processors was unthinkable when this monster was manufactured in the mid-1950s.

Five

At School
and at Play

Infants Class at the Norton School, 1911. This was the first purpose-built school to be opened at Letchworth. The children sit in rows at long narrow tables. The school mistress Edith Booth, was a cousin of Raymond Unwin.

Homemakers' Class, Norton School, 1910. The older girls learning domestic science are standing outside one of the grouped cottages on Birds Hill. Miss Booth stands in the centre of the group, but the smartly dressed school mistress in long pinafore and bow tie to the right is unidentified.

The St Christopher School had its origins in the Theosophy Movement, and the foundation stone was laid by Mrs Annie Besant in 1919 for the original premises built in the angle between Broadway and Spring Road (St Francis' College for Girls after 1934).

St Christopher's, well-known for its progressive teaching methods, provided open-air education on the broad verandah of the school. In 1934, the school moved to the Barrington Road buildings, originally constructed for the Letchworth School, where it remains.

Sports Day at the Westbury School, 1935. The school was opened in 1925 to cater for the children of the large council housing estate developed by Letchworth UDC. The race is taking place on the old playing fields south of West View, much of which were developed for housing in the late 1970s.

May Day at Hillshott School, 1924. This school used the buildings of the Pixmore Institute, which had been constructed as the Pixmore estate residents' club just before the First World War. In this charming picture, some of the boys, dressed as elves, look distinctly uncomfortable.

May festivities were a regular feature of Garden City life, with the annual ceremony of crowning the May Queen. Here, in 1906, the May Queen sits on a flower-decorated tuffet, surrounded by her attendants.

May Day 1912. Ebenezer Howard, and his second wife, are in the centre of the group.

Norton Common became the main recreation area of the town. Much of it was left in its original state, as shown in this 1912 view of one of its unspoilt byways.

The Common was brought into the Garden City Plan by creating a sweeping grass and tree-lined vista across it, continuing the axial line of Broadway to Wilbury Road. Little has changed from this early 1930s view.

Howard Park, lay in the valley of the Pix Brook, which was culverted to form Rushby Mead. In 1912 view, the grass is unmown, and the pool, dug by hand, is in its original state. In the background are the Mrs Howard Memorial Hall and Girls Club.

The Paddling Pool was created in 1930. A few years later, children dance around the fountain, while in the background are the brick screen walls flanking the Ebenezer Howard Memorial.

Reach for the sky. The Church Lads Brigade was one of many organisations providing recreation for local youths. In 1912 their gymnastic squad poses somewhat precariously.

By 1945, the Brigade met in Commerce Avenue, and had a smart, well turned-out band.

Works teams were a feature of Garden City sport: here the 1919-20 K&L Hockey Team poses with their female fans in the foreground.

Cycling was a popular recreation on the traffic-free roads before the Second World War: the British Tab Cycling Team of 1936 poses with its handsome trophy.

In 1910, before the First World War, tennis was considered to be a gentle game for demure young ladies.

The oval outdoor swimming pool at The Cloisters was in great demand for swimming lessons, and the formidable Miss Lawrence used to offer a prize of a fountain pen to those who successfully swam a length of its murky waters. In 1928, a young ladies' group poses with their tunic-clad coach.

As befitted a community where emphasis was placed on outdoor activities, the original swimming pool, south of Pixmore Way, now the Charles Ball Memorial Gardens, was a popular spot, despite being unheated.

THE SWIMMING POOL, LETCHWORTH.

G.4961.

Its successor, the open-air pool on Norton Common was opened in 1935. In the 1940s, it was well patronised and remains so, but the diving boards and chute have been removed at the insistence of Health and Safety officers.

The Skittles Inn, Nevells Road (now The Settlement) was built to provide local recreation, without the stigma of serving alcoholic refreshments. This fine Parker and Unwin building was a popular venue for recreation under the watchful eye of Bill Furmston in the pre-First World War period.

The Skittle Alley in 1909 and featured the ancestor of modern Ten Pin Bowling. The room was gas-lit, and darts and quoits were also available. The Settlement extended the alley in the 1950s as the Kincaid Hall.

Vegetarianism retained a strong, if minority following in Letchworth. In 1932, the Vegetarians Dinner was held in 'The People's House', Bill Furmston, originally 'mine host' at The Skittles, presides, left centre background.

Workers playtime. Cooper Bloomfield owned the earliest charabancs in Letchworth and ran day-trips to Southend and Clacton. This group in the 1920s, appears well-dressed to withstand the rigours of the open-air journey and the British summer.

The City Dance Band, c. 1925 (or 'The Temperance Five'!). Dance music and dancing were a popular recreation in the interwar period when local bands proliferated and recorded music was little used. Posed in 'The People's House', the players appear rather inhibited.

Ladies and Gentlemen of the chorus of Floradora from the Letchworth Operatic Society production of 1925 collectively smile for the camera.

Six

Home and Community

CARTOON No. 3.— WHAT SOME PEOPLE THINK OF US.

Two German ladies, who visited Letchworth last week, said on leaving :—" We are awfully disappointed in one thing : we were assured before coming that the people at Garden City were only half clothed, and that they all went bare-headed and wore sandals, and we have not seen one person of that sort ! "

It really is too bad of folks
 To come expecting something eerie,
We are just ordinary souls,
 The right-side up, not "tapsalteerie."

Our architect is harmless quite,
 *Un' win*some, too, at present,
Our di-*Rector* ap-*Pears* all smiles,
Our Agent, *Gaunt*—but pleasant.

'What some people think of us', 1909. Louis Weirter, a local artist, caught the spirit of the Garden City poking fun at itself in his cartoons. Here, a group from London have visited Letchworth to witness its mildly shocking free-thinking lifestyle. Dressed in smock and sandals, Walter Gaunt, Estate Manager, stands at the left offering factory sites for letting. On the right, Howard Pearsall digs his garden into which was fed the househoud effluent - no wonder the cabbages are flourishing. In the centre, Raymond Unwin is photographed at his drawing board.

Above: Home and garden - No 7 Willian Way, designed by Wilson Bidwell in 1907 as his family home. This beautifully laid out formal garden, with its sundial, reflects the qualities of the domestic architecture.

Right: Mrs Wilson Bidwell looks out of the house into the garden, a charming photograph taken by her architect-husband which encapsulates the spirit of life in the Garden City.

'Crabby Corner', the home of the architect Barry Parker. Situated in Letchworth Lane, the Parkers moved into half of a semi-detached pair, where Unwin had originally lived in the other half, 'Laneside'. In 1914, with a growing family, Parker added the distinctive three storey tower extension, with its sleeping porch on the top floor.

This view of the bedroom on the second floor hints at the spartan lifestyle of the pioneers, with windows open on all sides and only a small fireplace to generate warmth in winter. The handsome double bed, with bookshelves in the head, and fitted cupboards at the foot, was designed by Parker himself.

Gardening soon became a popular activity for all residents of Letchworth. This example has a natural look, being left mainly as a lawn, large enough for tennis, with shrub and herbaceous plants beneath the trees, and a more formal rose bed in the foreground.

Some gardens were elaborately landscaped. This fine example, overlooking Letchworth Lane, belonged to William Wallace Kincaid, founder of Spirella, and, in the early 1930s, was described as 'a sylvan scene ... within a few minutes walk of busy streets'.

Many early Garden City public buildings attained a serene Arts and Crafts character, none more so than Howgills, the Friends Meeting House, designed by Bennett and Bidwell in 1907, and built by Miss Juliet Reckitt who also lived there for several years.

The Meeting Room, photographed by Wilson Bidwell in 1910, has scarcely changed in the intervening eighty five years, and is a fine venue for musical events as well as the regular Meeting.

Workmens' cottages, Common View, built by Letchworth Cottages and Buildings Ltd, 1909-10. Among the most economical cottages built in Letchworth, these still provided three bedrooms, although the bath was in the scullery, and the lavatory outside.

Rear gardens, Hillshott and Pixmore Avenue, housing developed by the Howard Cottage Society Ltd, 1911-12, founded by Ebenezer Howard. Some of the finest working-class cottages in Letchworth, with gardens large enough to produce abundant vegetables, it appears that the builders have only recently moved away and the gardens have not yet been cultivated.

The Letchworth Parish Council in front of the Mrs Howard Memorial Hall, 1908. The Chairman, Sir John Gorst, sits front centre. Left to right: front row, C. F. Ball, E. Heatley, Sir John Gorst, D. B. Cockerell, George Brown; second row, J. S. Lander, C. Brown, R. J. E. Underwood, H. Hurst, H. C. Lander, T. Hudson, J. T. Openshaw; back row, N. MacFadyen, T. C. Howard, H. Hall, T. J. Godbehear.

The Letchworth Urban District Council was created in 1919. It will be noted that the 'official' name of the town, with 'Garden City' in parenthesis, is shown. Charles Ball, the Chairman, was a building contractor, long active in local affairs. The Clerk, George Brown, had negotiated many of the options on the land upon which Letchworth was built.

The Fire Brigade stand outside their original headquarters at New Farm on the Baldock Road. Shortly before the First World War they moved to new premises next door to the Picture Palace in Eastcheap.

The Fire Brigade hard at work to bring a blaze at one of the 'Noah's Ark' cottages on Birds Hill under control. Clearly, as the size of the crowd indicates, this was an exciting event. The horse-drawn fire cart is in the left foreground, while to the right, the local coal merchant appears to have stopped to observe the scene.

Esperanto, the International language, was seen as a basis for fostering cooperation between nations. In this conference, held in The Cloisters in June 1913, Ebenezer Howard sits immediately to the right of the policeman, and further right is Miss Annie Jane Lawrence, who had built The Cloisters as a centre for Theosophical education.

The hope for internationalism remained strong in the 1920s, as shown in this Co-operative Society pageant with its theme of bringing the nations together.

Ebenezer Howard had described Temperance as a 'local option'. Regular referenda were held, with universal suffrage. In the early 1920s, the main issue was whether a licensed restaurant should be allowed. Dr MacFadyen, well-known as a Parish and District Councillor and local physician for many years, was convinced that the town should remain dry.

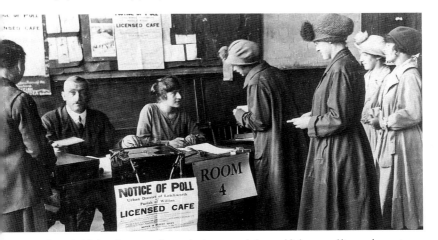

It was always held that the women's vote had prevented the establishment of licensed premises. The Broadway Hotel of the 1960s, introduced the first licensed cocktail bar, while the first public house in the town centre, The Black Squirrel, did not open until 1974.

The Coronation of King George V in 1911 was marked by a procession through the streets of Letchworth, led by Charles Ball, Chairman of the Parish Council on horseback. Beneath fluttering bunting and Union Jacks, the advance party moves up Station Road past 'Silver Birch' cottages.

Letchworth already had a sizeable elderly population in 1911, as shown in this photograph of the special Coronation tea party held in the Girls' Club wing of the Howard Hall. Everyone is dressed in their Sunday Best.

Ready to fight for King and Country, the young Territorials, stand on the up platform of Letchworth Station, 1914. Virtually as they left, an influx of Belgium refugees began arriving, as early as 25 September 1914, after the fall of Antwerp, and remained resident until 1919.

'The Letchworth Zeppelin'. On 2 and 3 September 1916 a lone Zeppelin flew over Hertfordshire as far north as Letchworth. Little damage was caused, but it was brought down over Cuffley near Potters Bar, where soldiers disposed of the wreckage.

Peace was celebrated by processions on the anniversary of Armistice Day, 11 November 1918. Spirella girls, draped in the flags of the Allies, who included Japan, parade in front of the partly completed factory. The scaffolding is in place for the final wing on the right.

A formal Armistice Day ceremony was held in the town centre. Soldiers guard a temporary Cenotaph, obviously modelled on that in London. In 1921, the permanent War Memorial in Station Place, designed by the local sculptor Onslow Whiting, was dedicated.

Interwar, Letchworth 'came of age'. This was the theme of Civic Week, held in 1926. Its main attraction was the first Royal visit to the Garden City. Here, Dr Norman MacFadyen welcomes HRH The Duke of York, later King George VI, on his arrival in Eastcheap.

Pioneers who moved to Letchworth before December 1908, and their children born in the Garden City, crowded the Icknield Halls on Saturday February 17 1934 to celebrate the 30th Anniversary of the Garden City. The gathering represented a 'who's who' of Garden City life and the residents' signatures were later worked into an embroidered cloth.

'Bombs-a-Daisy': heavy armaments from K&L included this 4,000 lb personalised present from Dulcie Dudley to the Fuhrer.

Best-known for their municipal refuse carts, Shelvoke and Drewry turned to the production of top secret miniature submarines used for naval espionage during the Second World War.

Dad's Army, the Home Guard, in a group photograph taken in 1940. The tape across the windows in the background was intended to minimize injury from shattered glass caused by bomb blasts. Fortunately, the Garden City sustained little damage.

'One of the few'. Letchworth Spitfire pilot J.G.P. (Joce) Millard, of the Nos 1, 242 and 615 Squadrons, photographed in 1940.

Macs and brollies are the uniform in June 1948 when Corner Close, old peoples bungalows built by the Howard Cottage Society, was opened. Seated at the table are, left, Nurse Webb, long remembered for her interest in old peoples welfare and Miss Kathleen M. Kaye, Manager of the Howard Cottage Society from 1944-67. Sir Eric MacFadyen, Chairman of First Garden City Ltd, sits on the front row facing the table.

With its landscaping completed, Corner Close, designed by John Tickle, could be seen as representing continuity in Garden City housing standards. In the 1940s, a start was also made on the ambitious UDC Grange Estate, which extended Letchworth northwards.

Seven

Time for Change

Mrs Amy Rose outside the Estate Office. In the late 1950s, First Garden City Limited, the original Development Company, became an attractive target for a takeover battle. The lady in the fur coat succeeded, through her London-based company, in purchasing the Garden City Estate as a whole.

Led by Ernest Gardiner, the residents of Letchworth publicly expressed their concern at the turn of events, and the Letchworth Urban District Council embarked upon a rescue campaign.

SAVE
Letchworth Garden City
PUBLIC MEETING
called by **ERNEST G. GARDINER**
THURSDAY DECEMBER 1 at 7.30 p.m.
GRAMMAR SCHOOL
Assembly Hall

The UDC Clerk, Horace Plinston, masterminded the drafting of a Private Parliamentary Act, to transfer the assets of the town from the private company to a public corporation. The campaign succeeded in 1962, with the passage of the Letchworth Garden City Corporation Act. Here, Cllr. William Askew presents Mr Plinston with a bound copy of the Act at the Civic Dinner held on 8 December 1962.

'What a dump', was the initial reaction of Robert Humbert, Chairman of the Letchworth Garden City Corporation, centre, to his Board colleagues and chief officers, left to right, John Barrett, unknown, John Ritchie, Laurie Freeman, Robert Humbert, Horace Plinston, Charles Sax and Leslie Bennett, to his left, as they moved into the First Garden City Company Offices in January 1963.

Presenting arms, March 1974. UDC Chairman, Charles Sax (centre) and Corporation Chairman, Robert Humbert (right) transfer the Letchworth UDC arms to the Corporation in advance of the formation of the North Hertfordshire District Council. Michael Kelly (left) originally Plinston's Deputy, was to become first Chief Executive of the new District Council.

Sir Frederic Osborn (left) and Robert Humbert at the 75th Anniversary Exhibition for Letchworth, July 1978. On one of his last public appearances, even though frail, Sir Frederic, long-time campaigner for Garden Cities and New Towns, made an impassioned speech about the significance of Letchworth.

Right: The Ernest Gardiner Day Hospital was one of the projects funded by the Corporation out of its operating surplus in the early 1980s. Here, the first matron, Mrs Jean Hyde, poses with one of her green-fingered day patients.

Below: Britannia rules the waves. The official opening of the North Herts Leisure Centre by HM Queen Elizabeth II, July 1982.

The run-down of long established industries in the early 1980s is underlined by this photograph, taken early in 1984, of the K&L land shortly before its redevelopment for the Business Park.

By October 1986, all had changed. Here, the Chief Executive of the Corporation, Andrew Egerton-Smith stands outside the newly completed Business Centre which marked the first phase of development on the Business Park.

Tree planting in the Business Park, March 1989: NHDC Chairman Alan Evens, and Corporation Chairman Sidney Melman.

Standalone Farm Visitor Centre became a most popular attraction from its opening in the early 1980s. Here David Marsh and Karen Morris, Miss Letchworth 1983, hold the reins of Warrant the Shire Horse, one of the centre's most popular attractions from 1980 until his death, aged 25 in 1993.

'But where can we put the parking ticket'. Bemused traffic wardens admire one of Roland Emmett's inimitable creations at the Corporation's 25th Anniversary Silver Jubilee Industrial Exhibition in 1987.

The Letchworth central area shopping centre, including a pedestrian precinct, multi-storey car park, and the North Hertfordshire District Council offices, had been built 1972-5, with major refurbishment in 1989. This eye-catching folly, a mixture of a traditional market cross and space probe, appeared briefly in the central square. Reputedly built in the wrong position, originally intended as a landmark to the Leys Avenue frontage, it disappeared without trace after a few months.

The answer lies in the soil. Rescue archaeology off Green Lane exposed the remains of an ancient settlement, tentatively known as 'Rodenhanger' before the site was redeveloped for housing.

The history man. The author, Mervyn Miller, signs a copy of his history of Letchworth for Margaret Bidwell, in David's Bookshop, December 1989.

Her Majesty the Queen arrives for the opening of Tabor Court Sheltered Housing, 30 July 1993. This included the 1000th home built by Howard Cottage Society. She unveiled a plaque, presented a commemorative key, and visited one of the flats.

Left: Outside the First Garden City Heritage Museum, Corporation Chairman Eric Lyall, exchanges gifts with Fujoka Shigehiero, leader of a group visit of Japanese Mayors, autumn 1993. Visits from Japanese city officials and planners have become increasingly popular in recent years.

Below: All change for Letchworth. The newly appointed Corporation Director General Stuart Kenny (left) and Station Manager Steve Newland with a new welcome sign to the First Garden City. In 1995, new legislation to form the Letchworth Garden City Heritage Foundation received Royal Assent, and the new body came into existence on 1 October 1995 – Foundation Day.

GREAT MEALS
WITH GROUND
MEAT

Consulting Editor:
Valerie Ferguson

southwater

Contents

Introduction

Ground meat is versatile, economical, goes a long way and is ideal for any number of quick and easy dishes. Nowadays, the range of ground meat available at butchers and supermarkets includes chicken, turkey, pork and lamb, as well as the more common ground beef, providing scope for an immense range of both traditional and more unusual dishes. With a meat grinder or food processor, it is easy to make your own ground meat and prepare other meat, fish and shellfish that are not commercially available.

This book is packed with ideas for family meals, snacks and light lunches, kids' dishes and even special occasions. Recipes range from traditional family favorites to more exotic dishes and include pies, fritters, pasta dishes and stuffed vegetables.

Ground meat combines well with many other ingredients, from herbs and spices to cheese and creamy sauces. No wonder it is featured in the cuisines of countries around the world, many of which have inspired the recipes in this book.

Whether you are planning a midweek family supper, entertaining on a budget or coping with a picky-eater, one of these many dishes based on ground meat will provide the solution.

Ingredients

Ground Beef:

This is the most widely available and popular ground meat. Obtainable in different grades, the most expensive, often labeled "ground steak" is usually the leanest. Some supermarkets supply "extra lean" or "premium quality" ground beef, but these terms have no legal meaning. Also, many supermarkets print nutritional information on the packaging

Ground Beef

material. Cheaper ground beef usually has a higher fat content — up to about 25 percent and about 12 percent saturated. It is, therefore, of poorer nutritional quality and not a smart buy. Ideally, buy steak in a single piece and grind it yourself.

Ground Pork:

Very popular in many Central European recipes, where it is often mixed with other types of ground meat, elsewhere pork is used less frequently. It is usually taken from one of the forequarter

Ground Pork

cuts and as these are comparatively lean, it is ideal for meatloaf or for stuffing vegetables. If a fattier cut is called for it is best to buy belly pork and grind it yourself.

Ground Lamb:

This is widely available and second to beef in popularity. It is usually taken from the neck, breast and flank. This is ideal for "lamb burgers" and other patties, but to avoid a high fat

Ground Lamb

content, it is better to buy the meat in one piece and grind it at home.

Ground Turkey & Chicken:

Virtually interchangeable in recipes, these are becoming increasingly popular. The fat content is considerably less than with red meat because most of the fat is removed with the skin. While less strongly flavored than ground beef, for example, ground turkey or chicken can be used

Ground Turkey

in most recipes that call for some sort of ground meat. They should be used on the day of purchase, as they quickly develop a slimy texture and get rancid. You can grind your own meat from turkey or chicken breasts or legs.

Herbs & Spices:

Both fresh and dried herbs can be used to enhance the flavor of ground meat dishes. Italian dishes, such as lasagne, benefit from oregano or marjoram. Basil is also widely used. Parsley

Basil

and thyme are good-all-purpose herbs. Tarragon is a popular choice for chicken and rosemary is the classic herb for flavoring lamb.

Chiles are essential in Mexican dishes and are also used in Indian and Southeast Asian cooking. There are many varieties ranging from fairly mild to fiery hot. You can remove the seeds from fresh chiles for a milder flavor. Chili powder is also often used in ground meat dishes. Other popular Indian spices include coriander and cumin.

Tarragon

Chili Powder

Cumin

Fresh ginger root is essential in Chinese, Southeast Asian and many Indian dishes.

Staple Ingredients:

Ground meat is perfect for making use of staple ingredients. These include dried or canned pulses and canned tomatoes. Dried apricots give ground lamb a Middle Eastern flavor. Both fresh and dried breadcrumbs can be added as a bulking agent or used to coat patties. Other bulking agents include bulghur wheat, rice and oatmeal. Useful staple flavorings are chili sauce, cranberry sauce, horseradish, mustard, soy sauce and ketchup.

Fresh Ingredients:

The range of fresh ingredients that complement ground meats is vast. Eggplant is essential in moussaka, and leeks, onions and scallions go well with all kinds of ground meat. Mushrooms, carrots and potatoes, as well as other root vegetables, are well-suited to many dishes featuring ground

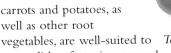

Tomatoes

meat. Fresh tomatoes are delicious in sauces and good for stuffing, as are bell peppers. Cheeses that melt well, such as Cheddar, Parmesan and mozzarella, make good toppings as do yogurt and sour cream.

Bell Peppers

Techniques

Grinding Meat

Ground meats are easily obtainable, but when you want something more unusual or to use a particular cut of meat, you will need to grind it yourself.

With a grinder:

1 This produces the most uniform ground meat, and you can choose coarse or fine textures, according to which blade is used. Trim and cut the meat into 1½-inch cubes or strips before feeding it through the machine.

By hand:

1 Trim the meat. Using a large knife, first cut the meat into cubes, then chop into smaller and smaller cubes. Continue chopping until you have the consistency you want, coarse or fine.

With a food processor:

1 Trim the meat carefully (be sure to remove all gristle because a food processor will chop gristle too) and cut it into cubes. Place in the machine fitted with the metal blade and pulse.

2 In between turning the machine on and off a few times, stir the meat around with a spatula so that it is evenly ground. Care must be taken not to over-process meat into a purée, particularly if making hamburgers, as they would be tough and chewy to eat.

Grinding Fish

Fish and shrimp are ideal for grinding in a food processor, using the chopping blade.

1 Wash, skin and bone the flesh.

2 Flake the fish and place in a food processor fitted with a chopping blade.

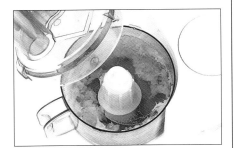

3 Process the fish for 30 seconds on high speed, or until finely ground. Use as required.

Basic Sauté

This cooking method forms the basis of many ground meat recipes. Meat is cooked in a small amount of oil to tenderize and seal in the flavors.

1 Heat a little oil in a heavy frying pan over medium heat for 1 minute.

2 Add the ground meat and sauté gently for 7 minutes.

3 Stir the meat, breaking it up with a wooden spoon, until it is brown and sealed.

Dry-frying

An alternative to the basic sauté, dry-frying is a healthier way to cook meats, as it does not require any additional fat or oil.

1 Heat a nonstick coated frying pan gently over low heat.

2 Add the ground meat. Sauté for 5 minutes, stirring and breaking it up with a wooden spoon, until brown and sealed.

Clear Soup with Meatballs

The tiny meatballs not only look attractive in this Indonesian soup, they also make it quite substantial and filling.

Serves 8

INGREDIENTS
1½ cups very finely
    ground beef
1 small onion, very finely chopped
1–2 garlic cloves, crushed
1 tablespoon cornstarch
a little egg white,
    lightly beaten
salt and freshly ground
    black pepper

FOR THE SOUP
4–6 Chinese mushrooms, soaked in warm
    water for 30 minutes
2 tablespoons peanut oil
1 large onion, finely chopped
2 garlic cloves, finely crushed
½-inch fresh ginger root, bruised
8 cups beef or chicken stock, including
    soaking liquid from the mushrooms
2 tablespoons soy sauce
4 ounces curly kale, spinach or
    Chinese cabbage, shredded

1 First, prepare the meatballs. Mix the beef with the onion, garlic, cornstarch and seasoning in a food processor and then bind with enough egg white to make a firm mixture. With wet hands, roll into tiny, bite-size balls and set aside.

2 Drain the mushrooms and reserve the soaking liquid to add to the stock. Trim off and discard the stems. Slice the caps finely and set aside.

3 Heat a wok or large saucepan and add the oil. Sauté the onion, garlic and ginger to bring out the flavor, but do not let it brown.

4 When the onion is soft, pour in the stock with the reserved soaking liquid from the mushrooms. Bring to a boil, then stir in the soy sauce and mushroom slices and simmer for 10 minutes. Add the meatballs and cook for 10 minutes.

5 Just before serving, remove the ginger. Stir in the shredded curly kale, spinach or Chinese cabbage. Heat through for 1 minute only but no longer, or the leaves will be over-cooked. Serve the soup immediately.

COOK'S TIP: Any unused fresh ginger root will keep very well in the freezer, provided it is left unpeeled and wrapped in freezer-foil or a freezer bag.

11

Meatball & Pasta Soup

This soup from sunny Sicily is substantial enough for a hearty supper.

Serves 4

INGREDIENTS
1 very thick slice of white bread,
   crusts removed
2 tablespoons milk
2 cups ground beef
1 garlic clove, crushed
2 tablespoons finely grated Parmesan cheese
2–3 tablespoons fresh flat-leaf
   parsley leaves, coarsely chopped
1 egg
nutmeg

FOR THE SOUP
2 11-ounce cans condensed
   beef consommé
scant 1 cup dried very thin pasta, broken into
   small pieces
fresh flat-leaf parsley, to garnish
freshly grated Parmesan cheese, to serve
salt and freshly ground black pepper

1 Make the meatballs. Break the bread into a small bowl, add the milk and set aside to soak. Put the ground beef, garlic, Parmesan, parsley and egg in another bowl. Grate nutmeg on top and season to taste.

2 Squeeze the bread with your hands to remove as much milk as possible, then add to the meatball mixture and mix well. Form the mixture into balls the size of small marbles.

3 Transfer the consommé to a large saucepan, add water as directed on the labels, then add an extra can of water. Season to taste and bring to a boil.

4 Drop in the meatballs and add the pasta. Bring to a boil, stirring gently. Simmer for 7–8 minutes. Serve hot sprinkled with parsley and Parmesan.

Nutty Chicken Balls

Serve as a first course with the sauce or make smaller balls for canapés.

Serves 4

INGREDIENTS
3 cups ground chicken
½ cup pistachios,
    finely chopped
1 tablespoon lemon juice
2 eggs, beaten
all-purpose flour, for shaping
¾ cup blanched chopped almonds
generous 1 cup dried bread crumbs
salt and freshly ground black pepper

FOR THE LEMON SAUCE
⅔ cup chicken stock
1 cup low-fat cream cheese
1 tablespoon lemon juice
1 tablespoon chopped fresh parsley
1 tablespoon snipped fresh chives

1 Make the meatballs. Mix the chicken with seasoning, the pistachios, lemon juice and one beaten egg.

2 Shape into 16 balls with floured hands. Roll the balls in the remaining beaten egg and coat with the almonds and then the dried bread crumbs. Chill until ready to cook.

3 Preheat the oven to 375°F. Place on a greased baking sheet and bake for about 15 minutes.

4 To make the lemon sauce, gently heat the chicken stock and cream cheese together in a pan, whisking until smooth. Add the lemon juice, herbs and season to taste.

Chicken Cigars

These small, crispy rolls can be served warm as canapés with a drink before a meal, or as a first course with a crisp, colorful salad.

Serves 4

INGREDIENTS
10-ounce package of phyllo pastry,
    thawed if frozen
3 tablespoons olive oil
fresh parsley, to garnish

FOR THE FILLING
1 tablespoon olive oil
1 small onion, finely chopped
3 cups ground chicken
1 egg, beaten
½ teaspoon ground cinnamon
½ teaspoon ground ginger
2 tablespoons raisins
salt and freshly ground
    black pepper

2 Preheat the oven to 350°F. Once the phyllo pastry package has been opened, keep the pastry covered at all times with a damp dish towel. Work fast, as the pastry dries out very quickly when exposed to the air. Unravel the pastry and cut into 4 x 10-inch strips.

1 Heat the oil for the filling in a large frying pan and cook the onion until tender. Set aside to cool. Meanwhile combine all the remaining filling ingredients in a bowl. Add the cooled onion to the mixture.

3 Take one strip, covering the remaining pastry. Brush with a little oil and place a small spoonful of filling about ½ inch from the end.

4 To encase the filling, fold the sides inward to a width of 2 inches and roll into a cigar shape. Place on a greased baking sheet and brush with oil. Bake for 20–25 minutes, until golden brown and crisp. Garnish with fresh parsley.

Lettuce-wrapped Garlic Lamb

For this tasty appetizer, lamb is stir-fried with garlic, ginger and spices, then served in crisp lettuce with yogurt, lime pickle and mint leaves.

Serves 4

INGREDIENTS
1 pound lamb fillet
½ teaspoon chili powder
2 teaspoons ground coriander
1 teaspoon ground cumin
½ teaspoon ground turmeric
2 tablespoons peanut oil
3–4 garlic cloves, chopped
1 tablespoon grated fresh
   ginger root
⅔ cup lamb stock or water
4–6 scallions, sliced
2 tablespoons chopped cilantro
1 tablespoon lemon juice
lettuce leaves, yogurt, lime pickle
   and mint leaves, to serve

2 In a bowl combine the chili powder, ground coriander, cumin and turmeric. Add the lamb and rub the spice mixture into the meat. Cover and let marinate for about 1 hour.

3 Heat the oil in a preheated wok. When hot, add the garlic and ginger and let sizzle for a few seconds.

1 Trim the lamb fillet of any fat and cut into small pieces, then grind in a blender or food processor, taking care not to over-process so that you retain some texture.

4 Add the lamb and continue to stir-fry for 2–3 minutes. Pour in the stock and continue to stir-fry until all the stock has been absorbed and the lamb is tender, adding a little more stock, if necessary.

5 Add the scallions, cilantro and lemon juice. Stir-fry for 30–45 seconds. Serve with the lettuce leaves, yogurt, pickle and mint leaves.

VARIATION: Vegetables, such as cooked diced potatoes or peas, can be added to the ground meat.

Dolmades

These dainty grape leaf parcels are very popular in Mediterranean countries. They are traditionally served as part of a Greek *mezze*.

Serves 4

INGREDIENTS
8 grape leaves
green and red bell pepper salad,
    to serve

FOR THE FILLING
1 tablespoon olive oil
1 cup ground beef
2 tablespoons pine nuts
1 onion, chopped
1 tablespoon chopped cilantro
1 teaspoon ground cumin
1 tablespoon tomato paste
salt and freshly ground
    black pepper

FOR THE TOMATO SAUCE
⅔ cup passata
⅔ cup beef stock
2 teaspoons sugar

1 For the filling, heat the oil in a pan. Add the ground beef, pine nuts and onion. Cook for 5 minutes.

2 Stir in the cilantro, cumin and tomato paste. Cook for another 3 minutes and season well.

3 Lay eight grape leaves shiny-side down on a work surface. Place some of the filling in the center of each leaf and fold the stalk end over the filling. Roll up the parcel toward the tip of the leaf and place in a lightly greased flameproof dish, seam-side down.

VARIATION: If grape leaves are unavailable, use lettuce or cabbage leaves blanched in boiling water until wilted.

4 For the sauce, combine the passata, stock and sugar and pour over each grape leaf. Cover and cook over medium heat for 3–4 minutes. Reduce the heat and cook for another 30 minutes. Serve with green and red pepper salad.

Fish Bites with Crispy Cabbage

Add an exotic element to a special meal with these attractive and tasty fish bites which are sure to impress.

Serves 4

INGREDIENTS
FOR THE FISH BITES
1½ cups peeled shrimp
12 ounces cod fillets
2 teaspoons light soy sauce
2 teaspoons sesame seeds
oil for deep-frying

FOR THE CABBAGE
8 ounces Savoy cabbage
pinch of salt
1 tablespoon sliced almonds
spring roll sauce, to serve

2 Roll the mixture into 16 even-size balls and toss in the sesame seeds to coat all over, pressing on firmly.

3 Heat the oil for deep-frying to 325°F. Shred the cabbage and place in the hot oil. Fry for 2 minutes. Drain well and keep warm. Sprinkle the cabbage with salt and toss in the sliced almonds.

1 Put the shrimp and cod in a food processor and process for 20 seconds. Place in a large bowl and stir in the soy sauce.

VARIATION: Any firm, white fish, such as haddock or whiting, would make a good substitute for cod.

4 Fry the balls in two batches for 5 minutes, until golden-brown. Remove with a draining spoon. Serve with the cabbage and some spring roll sauce for dipping.

Little Chicken Pies

These crisp little pies are equally delicious hot or cold and are perfect for packed lunches and picnics.

Makes 35

INGREDIENTS
2 cups all-purpose flour
½ teaspoon salt
½ teaspoon sugar
1 teaspoon active dry yeast
2 tablespoons butter, softened
1 egg, beaten, plus a little extra
6 tablespoons warm milk
fresh parsley, to garnish

FOR THE FILLING
1 small onion, finely chopped
1½ cups ground chicken
1 tablespoon sunflower oil
5 tablespoons chicken stock
2 tablespoons chopped fresh parsley
pinch of grated nutmeg
salt and freshly ground black pepper

1 Sift the flour, salt and sugar into a large bowl. Stir in the dried yeast, then make a well in the center.

2 Add the butter, egg and milk and mix into a soft dough. Turn onto a lightly floured surface and knead for 10 minutes, until smooth and elastic.

3 Put the dough in a clean bowl, cover with plastic wrap and set in a warm place to rise for 1 hour or until the dough has doubled in bulk.

4 Meanwhile, cook the onion and chicken in the oil for 10 minutes. Add the stock and simmer for 5 minutes. Stir in the parsley, nutmeg and salt and pepper. Let cool.

5 Preheat the oven to 425°F. Knead the dough, then roll out until ⅛ inch thick. Stamp out rounds with a 3-inch cutter.

VARIATION: Leftover Christmas turkey could be used instead of chicken—omit the nutmeg and add 1 tablespoon of curry paste with the parsley and seasoning.

6 Brush the edges with beaten egg. Put a little filling in the middle, then press the edges together. Let rise on oiled baking sheets, covered with oiled plastic wrap, for 15 minutes. Brush with a little more egg. Bake for 5 minutes, then for 10 minutes at 375°F, until well risen. Serve garnished with fresh parsley.

23

Dim Sum Dumplings

Popular as a Chinese snack, these tiny dumplings are fast becoming fashionable at many Chinese restaurants.

Serves 4

INGREDIENTS
FOR THE DOUGH
1¼ cups all-purpose flour
¼ cup boiling water
1½ tablespoons cold water
½ tablespoon vegetable oil

FOR THE FILLING
¾ cup ground pork
3 tablespoons chopped canned
    bamboo shoots
½ tablespoon light soy sauce
1 teaspoon dry sherry
1 teaspoon sugar
½ teaspoon sesame oil
1 teaspoon cornstarch

TO SERVE
lettuce leaves, such as iceberg
    or frisée
soy sauce
scallion curls
sliced red chile
shrimp crackers

3 For the filling, combine the pork, bamboo shoots, soy sauce, sherry, sugar and oil. Add the cornstarch.

4 Place a little of the filling in the center of each dumpling circle. Pinch the edges of the dough together to form little "purses."

VARIATION: Substitute the pork with cooked peeled shrimp. Sprinkle 1 tablespoon of sesame seeds onto the dumplings before cooking in a steamer.

1 For the dough, sift the flour into a bowl. Stir in the boiling water, then the cold water with the oil. Mix to form a dough and knead until smooth.

2 Divide the mixture into 16 equal-size pieces and shape each piece into a small circle.

5 Line a steamer with a damp dish towel. Place the dumplings in the steamer and steam for 5–10 minutes. Serve on a bed of lettuce with soy sauce, scallion curls, sliced red chile and shrimp crackers.

Indian Curried Lamb Samosas

In India, snacks are a way of life—sold from stalls lining the streets of towns and villages throughout the country.

Serves 4

INGREDIENTS
1 tablespoon oil
1 garlic clove, crushed
1½ cups ground lamb
4 scallions, finely chopped
2 teaspoons medium curry paste
4 dried apricots, chopped
1 small potato, diced
2 teaspoons apricot chutney
2 tablespoons frozen peas
dash of lemon juice
1 tablespoon chopped cilantro
8 ounces puff pastry, thawed if frozen
beaten egg, to seal and glaze
1 teaspoon cumin seeds
salt and freshly ground
    black pepper
3 tablespoons plain yogurt and
    1 tablespoon chopped fresh mint,
    to serve
fresh mint sprigs, to garnish

1 Preheat the oven to 425°F and dampen a large, nonstick baking sheet.

2 Heat the oil in a frying pan and cook the garlic for 30 seconds, then add the ground lamb. Continue frying for about 5 minutes, stirring frequently, until the meat is well browned.

3 Stir in the scallions, curry paste, apricots and potato, and cook for 2–3 minutes. Add the apricot chutney, peas and ¼ cup water. Cover and simmer for 10 minutes, stirring occasionally. Stir in the lemon juice and chopped cilantro. Season, remove from heat and let cool.

4 On a floured surface, roll out the pastry and cut into 6-inch squares. Place a quarter of the curry mixture in the center of each pastry square and brush the edges with beaten egg. Fold over to make a triangle and seal the edges. Seal the edges with the back of a knife and make a small slit in the top of each.

VARIATION: Phyllo pastry can be used instead of puff pastry; in which case, the samosas should be deep-fried in oil until golden-brown.

5 Brush each samosa with beaten egg and sprinkle on the cumin seeds. Place on the damp baking sheet and bake for 20 minutes. Serve with yogurt and mint and garnish with mint sprigs.

Spicy Meat Fritters

Quick and easy, these delicious fritters would make a light summer lunch, served with plain rice and salad.

Makes 30

INGREDIENTS

1 pound potatoes, boiled
   and drained
4 cups lean ground beef
1 onion, quartered
1 bunch scallions, chopped
3 garlic cloves, crushed
1 teaspoon ground nutmeg
1 tablespoon coriander seeds, dry-fried
   and ground
2 teaspoons cumin seeds, dry fried
   and ground
4 eggs, beaten
oil for shallow-frying
salt and freshly ground
   black pepper
cilantro leaves, to garnish

1 While the potatoes are still warm, mash them in the pan until they are well broken up. Add to the ground beef in a bowl and mix well together.

2 Finely chop the onion, scallions and garlic. Add to the ground beef mixture, together with the ground nutmeg, coriander and cumin. Stir in enough beaten egg to give a soft consistency, which can be formed into fritters. Season to taste with salt and pepper.

3 Heat the oil in a large frying pan. Using a teaspoon, scoop out 6–8 oval-shaped fritters and drop them into the hot oil. Let set, so that they keep their shape (this will take about 3 minutes) and then turn over and cook for another minute.

4 Drain well on paper towels and keep warm while cooking the remaining fritters. Serve hot, garnished with cilantro.

VARIATION: A mixture of half beef and half pork could be used instead of beef.

COOK'S TIP: Dry-frying whole spices helps to bring out their full aroma and flavor. Heat a heavy frying pan and add the coriander and cumin seeds. Fry, stirring constantly, for about 30 seconds, until the spices begin to release their aroma. Remove the pan from heat and let cool, then grind the seeds in a spice grinder, a coffee grinder kept expressly for this purpose or crush in a mortar with a pestle.

Ground Chicken with Chiles

This stir-fried dish is cooked in a matter of minutes and makes a very economical family supper.

Serves 4

INGREDIENTS
10 ounces boned and cubed
    skinless chicken breast
2 thick red chiles
3 thick green chiles
3 tablespoons corn oil
6 curry leaves
3 medium onions, sliced
1½ teaspoons crushed garlic
1½ teaspoons ground coriander
1½ teaspoons finely grated
    fresh ginger root
1 teaspoon chili powder
1 teaspoon salt
1 tablespoon lemon juice
2 tablespoons chopped fresh
    cilantro leaves
chapatis and lemon wedges, to serve

1 Boil the chicken cubes in water for about 10 minutes, until soft and cooked through. Drain.

2 Place the chicken in a food processor to grind. Take care not to over-process, or the chicken will become too pulpy.

3 Cut the chiles in half lengthwise and remove the seeds, if desired. Cut the flesh into strips.

4 Heat the oil in a wok or frying pan and sauté the curry leaves and onions until the onions are golden brown. Lower the heat; add the garlic, coriander, ginger, chili powder and salt.

5 Add the chicken and stir-fry over medium heat for 3–5 minutes, until the chicken begins to color.

COOK'S TIP: Taste this dish during cooking, as it is quite mild and may need additional spices to suit some palates.

6 Add the lemon juice, the chile strips and most of the cilantro leaves. Stir for another 3–5 minutes, then serve immediately, garnished with the remaining cilantro leaves and accompanied by chapatis and lemon wedges.

Lebanese Kibbeh

The national dish of Syria and the Lebanon is *kibbeh,* made from ground lamb and bulghur wheat.

Serves 6

INGREDIENTS
¾ cup bulghur wheat
4 cups finely ground lean lamb
1 large onion, grated
1 tablespoon melted butter
salt and freshly ground black pepper
sprigs of mint, to garnish
rice, to serve

FOR THE FILLING
2 tablespoons oil
1 onion, finely chopped
2 cups ground lamb or veal
½ cup pine nuts
½ teaspoon ground allspice

FOR THE YOGURT DIP
2½ cups plain yogurt
2–3 garlic cloves, crushed
1–2 tablespoons chopped fresh mint

1 Preheat the oven to 375°F. Rinse the bulghur wheat in a sieve and squeeze out excess moisture.

2 Mix the lamb, onion and seasoning, kneading to make a thick paste. Add the bulghur wheat and blend together.

3 To make the filling, heat the oil in a frying pan and sauté the onion until golden. Add the lamb or veal and cook, stirring, until evenly browned, and then add the pine nuts, allspice and salt and pepper.

4 Oil a large ovenproof dish and spread half the meat and bulghur wheat mixture on the bottom. Spoon on the filling and top with a second layer of meat and bulghur wheat, pressing down firmly with the back of a spoon.

5 Pour the melted butter on top and then bake for 40–45 minutes, until browned on top.

6 Meanwhile, make the yogurt dip: blend together the yogurt and garlic, spoon into a serving bowl and sprinkle with the chopped mint.

7 Cut the cooked *kibbeh* into squares or rectangles and serve garnished with mint and accompanied by rice and the yogurt dip.

Moussaka

Kefalotiri, a hard cheese made with sheep's or goat's milk, makes the
perfect topping for a classic moussaka.

Serves 6

INGREDIENTS
2 large eggplant, thinly sliced
3 tablespoons olive oil
6 cups lean ground beef
1 onion, chopped
2 garlic cloves, crushed
2 large fresh tomatoes, chopped, or
    7 ounces canned chopped tomatoes
½ cup dry white wine
3 tablespoons chopped fresh parsley
3 tablespoons fresh bread crumbs
2 egg whites
salt and freshly ground black pepper

FOR THE TOPPING
3 tablespoons butter
⅓ cup all-purpose flour
1⅔ cups milk
½ teaspoon freshly grated nutmeg
1¼ cups grated Kefalotiri cheese
2 egg yolks, plus 1 whole egg

1 Layer the eggplant slices in a
colander, sprinkling each layer with salt.
Drain over the sink for 20 minutes, then
rinse and pat dry with paper towels.

2 Preheat the oven to 375°F. Spread
out the eggplant slices in a roasting
pan. Brush them with olive oil, then
bake for 10 minutes, until just
softened. Remove and cool. Leave
the oven on.

3 Make the meat sauce. Heat the
remaining olive oil in a large saucepan
and brown the ground beef, stirring
frequently. When the meat is no longer
pink and looks crumbly, add the onion
and garlic and cook for 5 minutes.

4 Add the tomatoes to the pan and
stir in the wine. Season with salt and
pepper to taste. Bring to a boil, then
lower the heat, cover and simmer
for 15 minutes. Remove the pan
from heat, let cool for about
10 minutes, then stir in the chopped
parsley, fresh bread crumbs and the
egg whites.

5 Lightly grease a large ovenproof
dish, then spread out half the
eggplant in an even layer on the
bottom. Spoon on the meat sauce,
spread it evenly, then top with the
remaining eggplant.

6 To make the topping, put the butter, flour and milk in a saucepan. Bring to a boil over low heat, whisking constantly until the mixture thickens to form a smooth, creamy sauce. Lower the heat and simmer for 2 minutes. Remove the pan from heat, season, then stir in the nutmeg and half the cheese.

7 Cool for 5 minutes, then beat in the egg yolks and the whole egg. Pour the sauce over the eggplant topping and sprinkle with the remaining cheese. Bake for 30–40 minutes or until golden brown. Let the dish stand for 10 minutes before serving.

Stilton Burgers

Slightly fancier than the traditional burger, this tasty recipe contains a delicious surprise—lightly melted Stilton cheese encased in a juicy burger.

Serves 4

INGREDIENTS
4 cups ground beef
1 onion, finely chopped
1 celery stalk, chopped
1 teaspoon dried mixed herbs
1 teaspoon prepared mustard
½ cup crumbled Stilton cheese
4 burger buns
salt and freshly ground
   black pepper
salad and mustard pickle,
   to serve

1 Place the ground beef in a bowl, together with the onion and celery. Season well.

2 Stir in the herbs and mustard, bringing all the ingredients together to form a firm mixture.

3 Divide the mixture into eight equal portions. Place four on a cutting board and flatten each one slightly.

4 Place the crumbled Stilton cheese in the center of each, dividing it equally among them.

5 Flatten the remaining portions and place on top. Mold the mixture together encasing the crumbled cheese and shape into four burgers.

6 Broil under a medium heat for 10 minutes, turning once or until cooked through. Split the burger buns and place a burger and salad leaves inside each. Serve with salad and mustard pickle.

Spaghetti Bolognese

This dish is a popular classic at Italian restaurants everywhere.

Serves 4–6

INGREDIENTS
2 tablespoons olive oil
1 onion, finely chopped
1 garlic clove, crushed
1 teaspoon dried mixed herbs
¼ teaspoon cayenne pepper
3–4 cups ground beef
14-ounce can chopped Italian
    plum tomatoes
3 tablespoons ketchup
1 tablespoon sun-dried tomato paste
1 teaspoon Worcestershire sauce
1 teaspoon dried oregano
scant 2 cups beef stock
3 tablespoons red wine
14 ounces–1 pound dried spaghetti
salt and freshly ground black pepper
freshly grated Parmesan cheese, to serve

1 Heat the oil in a medium saucepan and cook the onion and garlic over low heat, stirring frequently, for about 5 minutes. Stir in the herbs and cayenne and cook for 2–3 minutes. Add the beef and cook, stirring frequently, for about 5 minutes.

2 Stir in the tomatoes, ketchup, tomato paste, Worcestershire sauce, oregano and pepper. Add the stock and red wine. Bring to a boil, stirring. Cover and simmer for 30 minutes, stirring often.

3 Cook the pasta according to the instructions on the package. Drain and divide among warmed bowls. Taste the sauce and adjust the seasoning, then spoon it on top of the pasta and sprinkle with a little grated Parmesan.

Bell Peppers with Ground Beef

Spicy ground beef makes a delightful filling for bell peppers.

Serves 4

INGREDIENTS
4 red bell peppers
1 onion
2 celery stalks
4 cups ground lean beef
¼ cup olive oil
2 ounces button mushrooms
pinch of ground cinnamon
salt and freshly ground black pepper
chervil or flat-leaf parsley,
    to garnish
green salad, to serve

1 Cut the tops off the peppers and reserve. Remove the seeds and membranes from the peppers. Finely chop the onion and celery. Set aside.

2 Sauté the ground beef in a nonstick frying pan for a few minutes, stirring until it is no longer red. Transfer the beef to a plate. Add half the oil to the pan and sauté the onion and celery over high heat until the onion starts to brown. Add the mushrooms and stir in the partly cooked beef. Season with the cinnamon, salt and pepper. Cook over low heat for about 30 minutes.

3 Preheat the oven to 375°F. Cut a sliver off the base of each pepper so they stand level, spoon in the beef mixture and replace the lids. Arrange in an oiled ovenproof dish, drizzle on the oil and cook for 30 minutes. Serve with green salad.

Cottage Pie

A great family favorite in England, cottage pie is almost a meal in itself and needs little in the way of accompanying vegetables.

Serves 4

INGREDIENTS
4 tablespoons butter
1 large onion, finely chopped
1 celery stalk, finely diced
1 large carrot, finely diced
4 cups lean ground beef
1 tablespoon all-purpose flour
1 cup hot beef stock
2 tablespoons chopped fresh parsley
1 tablespoon tomato paste
2 pounds floury potatoes
3–4 tablespoons milk
2 teaspoons spicy brown mustard
salt and freshly ground
    black pepper

2 Sprinkle the flour evenly on the surface and stir it into the meat and vegetable mixture.

3 Gradually add the stock, stirring well. Stir in the parsley and tomato paste. Season with salt and pepper. Bring to a simmer, then cover and cook over very low heat, stirring occasionally, for 45 minutes.

1 Melt 1 tablespoon of the butter in a frying pan over medium heat. Add the onion, celery and carrot and cook until the onion is soft, stirring occasionally. Add the beef and fry, stirring, until it is brown and crumbly.

VARIATION: For shepherd's pie, substitute lamb for beef. If time allows, prepare the ground beef and let cool before topping with the cooled mashed potatoes.

4 Meanwhile, cook the potatoes in boiling salted water until they are tender. Drain well. Transfer to a bowl and mash them. Add the remaining butter and just enough milk to make a soft fluffy texture. Season to taste with salt and pepper. Preheat the oven to 400°F.

5 Stir the mustard into the beef mixture, then transfer to an ovenproof dish. Cover with a layer of potatoes and seal to the sides of the dish. Mark with a fork, if desired. Bake for 20–25 minutes. Serve hot.

Meat Loaf with Mushroom Stuffing

This variation of the ever-popular meat loaf is just as filling, but has an extra touch of elegance.

Serves 6

INGREDIENTS

2 tablespoons butter
8 ounces mushrooms,
    coarsely chopped
1 small onion, finely chopped
2¼ cups fresh bread crumbs
3 tablespoons chopped fresh parsley
1 teaspoon dried thyme
2 teaspoons Worcestershire sauce
6 cups lean ground beef
2 cups lean ground pork
5 tablespoons ketchup
2 eggs, beaten
salt and freshly ground
    black pepper
flat-leaf parsley, to garnish
tomatoes and steamed asparagus,
    to serve (optional)

1 Preheat the oven to 375°F. Melt the butter in a large frying pan. Cook the mushrooms and onion in the butter over medium heat until soft. Transfer the mixture to a large bowl.

2 Add the bread crumbs, parsley, thyme, brown sauce, salt and pepper. Mix well.

3 In another bowl, mix the beef with the pork, ketchup and eggs.

4 Pack half the meat mixture into a large loaf pan, pressing it into an even layer. Pack the mushroom mixture on top, then cover with the rest of the meat. Bake for 1¼ hours.

5 Remove from the oven and let stand for 15 minutes. Pour off the juices, then turn out the meat loaf onto a serving plate. Garnish with parsley and serve with tomatoes and asparagus, if desired.

COOK'S TIP: Meat loaf is perfect for packed lunches or picnics, as when it is cold it can be cut into firm slices that go well with crusty bread and chutney or pickles.

Lasagne al Forno

This classic pasta dish is made with layers of lasagne, Bolognese sauce and a creamy béchamel sauce, topped with cheese.

Serves 4–6

INGREDIENTS
about 12 sheets dried lasagne
1 batch Bolognese sauce (see
    Spaghetti Bolognese)
about ½ cup freshly grated
    Parmesan cheese
tomato slices and parsley sprig, to garnish

BECHAMEL SAUCE
3¾ cups milk
sliced onion, carrot, celery
few whole peppercorns
¼ cup butter
⅔ cup all-purpose flour
freshly grated nutmeg
salt and freshly ground
    black pepper

1 First, make the béchamel sauce. Pour the milk into a saucepan and add the vegetables and peppercorns. Bring to the boiling point, remove from heat and set aside to infuse for at least 30 minutes.

2 Strain the milk into a pitcher. Melt the butter in the saucepan and stir in the flour. Cook, stirring, for 2 minutes.

3 Remove from heat and add the milk at once, whisk well and return to the heat. Bring to a boil, whisking constantly, then simmer for 2–3 minutes, stirring until thickened. Season to taste with salt, pepper and nutmeg.

4 Preheat the oven to 350°F. If necessary, cook the sheets of lasagne in plenty of boiling salted water according to the instructions. Lift out with a slotted spoon and drain on a clean dish towel. Spoon one-third of the meat sauce into a buttered ovenproof dish.

5 Cover the meat sauce with four sheets of lasagne and spread with one-third of the béchamel sauce. Repeat twice more, finishing with a layer of béchamel sauce covering the whole top.

6 Sprinkle with Parmesan cheese and bake for 45 minutes, until brown. Serve garnished with tomato slices and a sprig of parsley.

45

Fish Balls with Chinese Greens & Snowpeas

These tasty fish balls are easy to make using a food processor. Here, they are partnered with a selection of green vegetables.

Serves 4

INGREDIENTS
FOR THE FISH BALLS
1 pound white fish fillets, skinned,
    boned and cubed
3 scallions, chopped
¼ pound bacon, chopped
1 tablespoon Chinese rice wine
2 tablespoons light soy sauce
1 egg white
cilantro, to garnish

FOR THE VEGETABLES
1 small head bok choy
1 teaspoon cornstarch
1 tablespoon light soy sauce
⅔ cup fish stock
2 tablespoons peanut oil
2 garlic cloves, sliced
1-inch piece fresh ginger root,
    cut into thin shreds
3 ounces green beans
6 ounces snowpeas
3 scallions, sliced diagonally into
    2–3-inch lengths
salt and freshly ground black pepper

1 Put the fish, scallions, bacon, rice wine, soy sauce and egg white in a food processor. Process until smooth. With wetted hands, form the mixture into about 24 small balls.

2 Steam the fish balls in batches in a lightly greased bamboo steamer set over a wok for 5–10 minutes, until firm. Remove from the steamer and keep warm.

3 Meanwhile, trim the bok choy, removing any discolored leaves or damaged stems, then tear into manageable pieces.

4 In a small bowl blend together the cornstarch, soy sauce and stock into a smooth paste. Set aside.

5 Heat the oil in a preheated wok and swirl it around. Add the garlic and ginger and stir-fry for 1 minute. Add the beans and stir-fry for 2–3 minutes, then add the snowpeas, scallions and bok choy. Stir-fry for 2–3 minutes.

6 Add the sauce to the wok and cook, stirring, until it has thickened and the vegetables are tender but crisp. Taste and adjust the seasoning, if necessary. Serve with the fish balls, garnished with cilantro.

Chicken & Apricot Phyllo Pie

The filling for this pie has a Middle Eastern flavor—ground chicken combined with apricots, bulghur wheat, nuts and spices.

Serves 6

INGREDIENTS
½ cup bulghur wheat
6 tablespoons butter
1 onion, chopped
4 cups ground chicken
¼ cup dried apricots, finely chopped
¼ cup blanched almonds, chopped
1 teaspoon ground cinnamon
½ teaspoon ground allspice
¼ cup plain yogurt
1 tablespoon snipped fresh chives
2 tablespoons chopped fresh parsley
6 sheets phyllo pastry,
    thawed if frozen
salt and freshly ground black pepper
chives, to garnish

1 Preheat the oven to 400°F. Put the bulghur wheat in a bowl with ½ cup boiling water. Soak for 5–10 minutes, until the water is absorbed. Heat 2 tablespoons of butter and cook the onion and chicken until pale golden.

2 Stir in the apricots, almonds and bulghur wheat and cook for another 2 minutes. Remove from heat and stir in the cinnamon, allspice, yogurt, chives and parsley. Season to taste with salt and pepper.

3 Melt the remaining butter. Unroll the phyllo pastry and cut into 10-inch rounds. Keep the pastry rounds covered with a clean, damp dish towel to prevent them from drying out.

4 Line a 9-inch loose-based tart pan with three of the pastry rounds, brushing each one with butter as you layer them. Spoon in the chicken mixture, and cover with three more pastry rounds, brushing each round with melted butter as before.

VARIATION: You could use other dried fruit in this pie. Figs or dates would make an interesting alternative to the apricots.

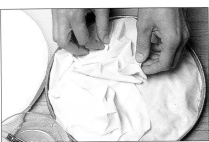

5 Crumple the remaining rounds and place them on top of the pie, then brush on any remaining melted butter. Bake the pie for about 30 minutes, until the pastry is golden brown and crisp. Serve hot or cold, cut into wedges and garnished with chives.

Risotto

An Italian dish made with short grain arborio rice, which gives a creamy consistency to this easy one-pan recipe.

Serves 4

INGREDIENTS
1 tablespoon oil
1½ cups arborio rice
1 onion, chopped
2 cups ground chicken
2½ cups chicken stock
1 red bell pepper, seeded and chopped
1 yellow bell pepper, seeded
    and chopped
3 ounces frozen green beans
4 ounces chestnut mushrooms, sliced
1 tablespoon chopped fresh parsley
salt and freshly ground
    black pepper
fresh parsley, to garnish

1 Heat the oil in a large frying pan. Add the rice and cook for 2 minutes, until transparent.

2 Add the onion and ground chicken. Cook for 5 minutes, stirring occasionally. Pour in the stock and bring to a boil. Stir in the peppers and reduce the heat. Cook for 10 minutes.

3 Add the green beans and mushrooms and cook for another 10 minutes.

4 Stir in the fresh parsley and season well to taste. Cook for 10 minutes or until the liquid has been absorbed. Serve, garnished with fresh parsley.

Cèpe Meatballs

The rich acidity of Roquefort sauce enhances the flavor of good beef.

Serves 4

INGREDIENTS
¼ cup dried cèpes, soaked in
    warm water for 20 minutes
4 cups lean ground beef
1 small onion, finely chopped
2 egg yolks
2 teaspoons chopped fresh thyme
2 tablespoons olive oil
celery salt and freshly ground black pepper
ribbon pasta, to serve

FOR THE ROQUEFORT SAUCE
scant 1 cup milk
½ cup walnuts, toasted
3 slices white bread, crusts removed
3 ounces Roquefort cheese
¼ cup chopped fresh parsley

1 Drain the mushrooms, reserving the liquid, and chop finely. Place the beef, onion, egg yolks, thyme and seasoning in a bowl, add the mushrooms and combine. Divide into small pieces with wet hands and roll into balls.

2 Make the sauce. Place the milk in a pan and bring to a simmer. Grind the walnuts in a food processor, add the bread, milk, reserved liquid, cheese and parsley, then process smoothly. Transfer to a bowl, cover and keep warm.

3 Heat the olive oil in a large nonstick frying pan. Cook the meatballs for 6–8 minutes. Add the sauce and heat gently, without letting boil. Serve with ribbon pasta.

Meatballs with Peperonata

These taste very good with creamed potatoes. Use a potato ricer to get them really smooth.

Serves 4

INGREDIENTS
3½ cups ground beef
2 cups fresh white bread crumbs
⅔ cup grated Parmesan cheese
2 eggs, beaten
pinch of paprika
pinch of grated nutmeg
1 teaspoon dried mixed herbs
2 thin slices of mortadella or prosciutto (total weight about 2 ounces), chopped
vegetable oil, for shallow-frying
salt and freshly ground black pepper
snipped fresh basil leaves, to garnish

FOR THE PEPERONATA
2 tablespoons olive oil
1 small onion, thinly sliced
2 yellow bell peppers, cored, seeded and cut lengthwise into thin strips
2 red bell peppers, cored, seeded and cut lengthwise into thin strips
1¼ cups finely chopped tomatoes or passata
1 tablespoon chopped fresh parsley

1 Put the ground beef in a bowl. Add half the bread crumbs and all the remaining ingredients, including salt and ground black pepper to taste. Mix well with clean wet hands. Divide the mixture into 12 equal portions and roll each into a ball. Flatten the meatballs so they are about ½ inch thick.

2 Put the remaining bread crumbs on a plate and roll the meatballs in them, a few at a time, until they are evenly coated. Place on a plate, cover with plastic wrap and chill for about 30 minutes to firm.

3 Meanwhile, make the peperonata. Heat the oil in a medium saucepan, add the onion and cook gently for about 3 minutes, stirring frequently, until softened. Add the pepper strips and cook for another 3 minutes, stirring constantly.

4 Stir in the tomatoes or passata and parsley, with salt and pepper to taste. Bring to a boil, stirring. Cover and cook for 15 minutes, then remove the lid and continue to cook, stirring frequently, for 10 minutes more or until reduced and thick. Taste for seasoning. Keep hot.

5 Pour oil into a frying pan to a depth of about 1 inch. When hot but not smoking, shallow-fry the meatballs for 10–12 minutes, turning them 3–4 times and pressing them flat with a spatula. Remove and drain on paper towels. Serve hot, with the peperonata alongside. Garnish with the basil.

Lion's Head Meatballs

These larger-than-usual pork meatballs are first fried, then simmered in stock. They are traditionally served with a fringe of greens, such as bok choy, to represent the lion's mane.

Serves 2–3

INGREDIENTS

4 cups lean pork, ground finely
   with a little fat
4–6 drained canned water chestnuts,
   finely chopped
1 teaspoon finely chopped
   fresh ginger root
1 small onion, finely chopped
2 tablespoons dark soy sauce
beaten egg, to bind
2 tablespoons cornstarch, seasoned with salt
   and freshly ground black pepper
2 tablespoons peanut oil
1¼ cups chicken stock
½ teaspoon sugar
4 ounces bok choy, stems trimmed
   and the leaves rinsed
salt and freshly ground black pepper

1 Mix the pork, water chestnuts, ginger and onion with 1 tablespoon of the soy sauce in a bowl. Add salt and pepper to taste, stir in enough beaten egg to bind, then form into eight or nine balls. Toss a little of the cornstarch into the bowl and make a paste with the remaining cornstarch and water.

2 Heat the oil in a large frying pan and brown the meatballs all over. Using a slotted spoon, transfer the meatballs to a wok or deep frying pan.

3 Add the stock, sugar and the remaining soy sauce to the oil that is left in the pan. Heat gently, stirring to incorporate the sediment on the bottom of the pan. Pour onto the meatballs, cover and simmer gently for 20–25 minutes.

4 Increase the heat and add the bok choy. Continue to cook for 2–3 minutes or until the leaves are just wilted.

5 Lift out the greens and arrange on a serving platter. Top with the meatballs and keep hot. Stir the cornstarch paste into the sauce. Bring to a boil, stirring, until it thickens. Pour onto the meatballs and serve immediately.

VARIATION: Crabmeat or shrimp can be used instead of some of the pork in this recipe. Alternatively, you could try substituting ground lamb or beef for the pork used here.

55

Fish Cakes

For extra-special fish cakes, you could use cooked fresh salmon.

Serves 4

INGREDIENTS

15⅓ cups cooked,
    mashed potatoes
4 cups cooked mixed white
    and smoked fish such as haddock
    or cod, flaked
2 tablespoons butter, diced
3 tablespoons chopped fresh parsley
1 egg, separated
1 egg, beaten
about scant 1 cup fine
    dry bread crumbs
vegetable oil, for frying
freshly ground black pepper
mixed salad, to serve

1 Place the potatoes in a bowl and beat in the fish, butter, parsley and egg yolk. Season with pepper.

2 Divide the fish mixture into eight equal portions, then, with floured hands, form each into a flat cake.

3 Beat the remaining egg white with the whole egg. Dip each fish cake in the beaten egg, then in bread crumbs.

4 Heat the oil in a frying pan, then fry the fish cakes for about 3–5 minutes on each side, until crisp and golden. Drain on paper towels and serve hot with a mixed salad.

Best-ever Burgers

Once you have tried homemade burgers you will never want any others.

Serves 4

INGREDIENTS

1 tablespoon vegetable oil
1 small onion, finely chopped
4 cups ground beef
1 large garlic clove, crushed
1 teaspoon ground cumin
2 teaspoons ground coriander
2 tablespoons tomato paste or ketchup
1 teaspoon whole-grain mustard
dash of Worcestershire sauce
2 tablespoons chopped fresh mixed herbs
    (parsley, thyme and oregano or marjoram)
1 tablespoon lightly beaten egg
all-purpose flour, for shaping
oil, for frying (optional)
salt and freshly ground black pepper
mixed salad, chips and relish, to serve

1 Heat the oil in a frying pan, add the onion and cook for 5 minutes. Remove from the pan, drain on paper towels and let sit.

2 Combine the beef and next eight ingredients. Season to taste. Stir in the onions.

3 Sprinkle a board with flour and shape the mixture into four burgers. Cover and chill for 15 minutes.

4 Heat the oil in a pan and fry the burgers for about 5 minutes on each side, depending on how rare you like them, or cook under a medium broiler for the same time. Serve with salad, chips and relish.

Köfte in Pita Pockets

Köfte is the Turkish name for meatballs. These are made with ground lamb and flavored with cumin.

Serves 4

INGREDIENTS

1 slice bread
2 cups ground lamb
1 garlic clove, crushed
1 small onion, finely chopped
1 teaspoon ground cumin
1 tablespoon chopped fresh mint
1 tablespoon pine nuts
all-purpose flour for coating
oil for shallow-frying
4 pita breads
1 onion, cut into thin rings
2 tomatoes, sliced or cut
   into wedges
salt and freshly ground black pepper
fresh mint, to garnish

1 Preheat the oven to 425°F. Soak the bread in water for 5 minutes, then squeeze dry and add the next six ingredients. Season. Mix until blended and malleable. Shape into small balls, using dampened hands so that the mixture does not stick. Coat in flour.

2 Shallow-fry the köfte in oil for about 6 minutes, turning frequently, until golden brown.

3 Heat the pita breads in the oven, then cut a thin strip off one side to make a pocket. Fill each bread with onion rings, tomato wedges and a few köfte. Serve garnished with mint.

Mexican Tacos

Ready-made taco shells make perfect edible containers for shredded salad, meat fillings, grated cheese and sour cream.

Serves 4

INGREDIENTS
1 tablespoon olive oil
generous 2 cups lean ground
    beef or turkey
1 garlic clove, crushed
1 teaspoon ground cumin
1–2 teaspoons mild chili powder
8 ready-made taco shells
½ small iceberg lettuce, shredded
1 small onion, thinly sliced
2 tomatoes, chopped in chunks
1 avocado, halved, pitted
    and sliced
¼ cup sour cream
1 cup grated Cheddar or Monterey
    Jack cheese
salt and freshly ground black pepper

1 Heat the oil in a frying pan. Add the meat, with the garlic and spices, and brown over medium heat, stirring frequently to break up any lumps. Season, cook for 5 minutes, then set aside to cool slightly.

2 Meanwhile, warm the taco shells according to the instructions on the package. Do not let them get too crisp. Spoon the lettuce, onion, tomatoes and avocado slices into the taco shells. Top with the sour cream followed by the ground beef or turkey mixture.

3 Sprinkle the cheese into the tacos and serve immediately. Tacos are eaten with the fingers, so have plenty of paper napkins handy.

Popovers

A lot of fun and very delicious, these individual corn-filled popovers are filled with tasty meatballs and then baked.

Serves 4

INGREDIENTS
½ cup all-purpose flour
pinch of salt
1 egg
⅔ cup milk
½ cup canned corn, drained
1 tablespoon butter
cooked vegetables, baked beans or salad,
    to serve

FOR THE FILLING
1 cup ground beef
1 red onion, chopped
2 tablespoons tomato relish
1 cup fresh whole-wheat
    bread crumbs
1 tablespoon oil
salt and freshly ground
    black pepper

1 Preheat the oven to 425°F. For the batter, sift the flour and salt into a mixing bowl. Make a well in the center.

2 Whisk the egg into the flour mixture, add the milk gradually to form a smooth batter. Add the corn.

3 For the filling, place the ground beef in a large bowl. Add the onion and seasoning.

4 Stir in the tomato relish and bread crumbs and bring the mixture together. Roll into four balls.

5 Heat the oil in a large pan and fry the meatballs to seal. Place the butter in a four-section popover pan and put into the preheated oven until melted.

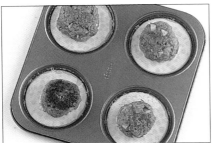

6 Divide the batter among each section of the pan and place a meatball in the center of each. Cook for 30 minutes. Remove from the oven and serve with freshly cooked vegetables, baked beans or a salad.

Beef Patties

These meat and vegetable filled parcels may be made in advance and frozen.

Serves 8

INGREDIENTS

1 tablespoon oil
1½ cups ground beef
1 tablespoon tomato paste
1 onion, chopped
1 carrot, diced
2 ounces turnip, diced
1 large potato, diced
¼ cup all-purpose flour
⅔ cup beef stock
1 tablespoon chopped
   fresh parsley
1 pound prepared shortcrust pastry
1 egg, beaten
salt and freshly ground
   black pepper
salad, to serve

2 Stir in the flour and cook for 1 minute. Stir in the stock and season to taste. Cook over low heat for 10 minutes. Stir in the fresh parsley and let cool.

3 Roll out the pastry to a large rectangle. Cut eight 6-inch circles, using a bowl or saucer as a template.

1 Preheat the oven to 375°F. Heat the oil in a large pan and add the ground beef. Cook for 5 minutes. Stir in the tomato paste, onion, carrot, turnip and potato. Cook for another 5 minutes.

VARIATION: For a more gamey flavor, use the same amount of ground rabbit instead of the beef and substitute sliced celery for the turnip. Replace the beef stock with dry cider.

4 Spoon the filling onto one half of each pastry circle, brush the edges with egg and fold in half to form a semi-circle. Crimp the edges and roll. Brush the pasties with egg and place on a baking sheet. Cook for 35 minutes or until golden. Serve with a crisp salad.

This edition published by Southwater

Distributed in the UK by
The Manning Partnership, 251-253 London Road East,
Batheaston, Bath BA1 7RL, UK
tel. (0044) 01225 852 727 fax. (0044) 01225 852 852

Distributed in Australia by
Sandstone Publishing, Unit 1, 360 Norton Street,
Leichhardt, New South Wales 2040, Australia
tel. (0061) 2 9560 7888 fax. (0061) 2 9560 7488

Distributed in New Zealand by
Five Mile Press NZ, PO Box 33-1071,
Takapuna, Auckland 9, New Zealand
tel. (0064) 9 4444 144 fax. (0064) 9 4444 518

Southwater is an imprint of Anness Publishing Limited

© 2000 Anness Publishing Limited

Publisher: Joanna Lorenz
Editor: Valerie Ferguson
Series Designer: Bobbie Colgate Stone
Designer: Andrew Heath
Editorial Reader: Diane Ashmore
Production Controller: Joanna King

1 3 5 7 9 10 8 6 4 2

Printed and bound in Singapore

Recipes contributed by: Catherine Atkinson,
Angela Boggiano, Lesley Chamberlain,
Maxine Clarke, Trisha Davies, Roz Denny,
Joanna Farrow, Sarah Gates, Shirley Gill,
Carole Handslip, Deh-Ta Hsuing, Shehzad Husain,
Judy Jackson, Soheila Kimberley,
Norma MacMillan, Sue Maggs, Sallie Morris,
Jenny Stacey, Hilaire Walden, Steven Wheeler,
Jeni Wright.

Photography: Edward Allwright, Steve Baxter,
Mickie Dowie, James Duncan, Ian Garlick,
Michelle Garrett, John Heseltine,
Amanda Heywood, Ferguson Hill,
Janine Hosegood, David Jordan,
William Lingwood, Patrick McLeavey.